ORIGINAL INTENT

ORIGINAL INTENT

Chief Justice Rehnquist
and the Course of
American Church/State Relations

DEREK DAVIS
Foreword by *Leo Pfeffer*

Prometheus Books
Buffalo, New York

6/99

22907518

Published 1991 by Prometheus Books

95 94 93 92 91   5 4 3 2 1

Library of Congress Cataloging-in-Publication Data

Davis, Derek, 1949-
    Original intent: Chief Justice Rehnquist and the course of American church-state relations / by Derek Davis.
        p.   cm.
    Includes bibliographical references and index.
    ISBN 0-87975-649-7
    1. Freedom of religion—United States. 2. United States—Constitutional law—Amendments—1st. 3. Rehnquist, William H., 1924-   . 4. United States. Supreme Court. 5. Church and state—United States. I. Title.
KF4783.D38   1991
342.73'9852—dc20
[347.302852]   90-27447
                                                                            CIP

Printed in the United States of America on acid-free paper.

To my favorite people:
Kim, my wife,
and Jeff and Melanie, my children

CONTENTS

FOREWORD

by Leo Pfeffer

Derek Davis joins a long line of supporters of religious liberty and separation of church and state, which began with Thomas Jefferson and James Madison. Davis meets here with Chief Justice William Rehnquist, currently the most influential spokesman for those who would leave it to the federal and state legislatures to follow or abandon these principles as they choose.

We owe the phrase "separation of church and state" to Thomas Jefferson. Jefferson had long been deeply concerned with problems of religious liberty, and, once elected President, looked for an opportunity to express his views formally. The occasion came in connection with thanksgiving celebrations. As Davis points out, Jefferson's predecessors, Presidents Washington and Adams, had felt no compunction in proclaiming fastings and thanksgivings. To Jefferson, these were not consistent with a constitution that mandated the separation of church and state, but there was no easy way of telling this to the people of the States. By chance, along came a letter from a committee of the Danbury Baptist Association. Jefferson explained to his Attorney General, Levi Lincoln, that the response "furnishes an occasion, too, which I have long wished to find, of saying why I do not proclaim fastings and thanksgivings, as my predecessors did." Seizing his opportunity, Jefferson drafted a now-famous letter stating that in writing the First Amendment, which forbade laws respecting an establishment of religion, the people were building a "wall of separation between church and state."

This phrase, like the philosophy it espouses, seems to enrage the Chief Justice. "The 'wall of separation between church and state,' " Rehnquist has written, "is a metaphor based on bad history, a metaphor which has proved useless as a guide to judging. It should be frankly and explicitly abandoned." Moreover, he said, Jefferson was in France when the first ten amendments (especially the first) were adopted by Congress and the States, and therefore cannot be relied upon in determining what they were intending to mean.

To this it might be responded that even in France Jefferson was closer to these events than any Supreme Court Justice in the late twentieth century can hope to be. In any event, Derek Davis provides a clear account of the importance of the Virginia experience and of the views of Jefferson and Madison in the development of American thought on church and state that was embodied in the First Amendment.

It is worth remembering that the idea of a wall of separation between church and state is older than Jefferson's use of the phrase. More than a century and a half before Jefferson's letter, Roger Williams of Rhode Island wrote his own famous letter, to the Town of Providence, describing a ship in which the captain commands the ship and the seamen in secular matters, but the seamen and passengers can separate themselves, "papists, protestants, Jews and Turks," and pray if they wish. The concept also appears in the widely read revolutionary pamphlet *Common Sense,* where Thomas Paine wrote: "As to religion, I hold it to be the indispensable duty of government to protect all conscientious professors thereof, and I know of no other business which government hath to do therewith." Jefferson did not invent the separation of church and state in the United States, nor was his support of it based on "bad history."

Davis also calls attention to the relation between separation of church and state and religious liberty. Many opponents of separation, including Rehnquist himself, have accused separationists of hostility to religion. Proponents of mandated prayers in public schools, or of financial aid to religious schools, for example, have charged separationist opposition to these policies as being simply antireligious, and have welcomed Rehnquist's defense of the constitutionality of these measures. In fact, as Davis explains, Rehnquist's position on these matters is governed by his willingness to endorse legislative decisions, whatever they may be, and not by any special sympathy for religious liberty. It is the separationists who are the consistent defenders of the free exercise of religion.

Davis properly devotes almost a full chapter to the case of *Employment Division, Department of Human Resources of Oregon* v. *Smith*, although the opinion in the case was actually written by Justice Antonin Scalia. Nevertheless, Rehnquist joined in the opinion, which clearly reflects the views he had set forth in earlier dissenting opinions.

The case dealt with two members of the Native American Church who injested peyote as part of a religious ceremony and were fired from their jobs because of this "misconduct." (When Prohibition was in effect, religious Catholics and religious Jews were allowed to engage in drinking wine as required by religious law. Many states, but not Oregon, allow similar privileges to members of the Native American Church.) Under Oregon law, the two had lost not only their jobs but also their right to receive unemployment compensation.

Oregon's Supreme Court then ruled that denial of unemployment compensation violated the Free Exercise Clause of the First Amendment and therefore was impermissible. This result was unsurprising. A whole line of cases had seemed to establish the proposition that denying someone unemployment benefits because of his religious practices violated the Constitution unless there was a compelling state interest involved.

Then came the Supreme Court's ruling on the case in April 1990. The Court held that the Free Exercise Clause of the First Amendment did not prohibit application of Oregon's drug laws to the religious ceremonial use of peyote and that Oregon could constitutionally deny the peyote users unemployment compensation. In essence, the Court held that the Free Exercise Clause is irrelevant to statutes that restrict religious liberty so long as they are general laws and not aimed specifically at a religious practice. So a law forbidding Catholics to carry rosary beads in a public park would violate their religious freedom, but not a law prohibiting all kinds of beads.

Derek Davis is entirely right in noting that the *Smith* decision "surprised everyone—liberals and conservatives alike" and that "it was difficult to find anyone—liberals or conservatives—happy about the decision's potential impact on religious liberty." Thus James E. Wood, Jr., one of the nation's leading experts in the area of church-state relations in the United States and throughout the world, editorialized in the Autumn 1990 issue of the *Journal of Church and State* that "the *Smith* decision, no matter what justification may be advanced by its defenders, constitutes a substantial abridgment of the free exercise of religion." A diverse coalition of religious and secular organizations and leading constitutional lawyers petitioned the Supreme Court for a rehearing, in essence asking the Court to take back what it had done. The Court denied the petition. I suspect many of Chief Justice Rehnquist's religious admirers are having second thoughts since the *Smith* decision. As Davis makes clear, though, the *Smith* opinion is entirely consistent with Rehnquist's earlier positions. The separationists on the Court—Justices Brennan, Marshall, and Blackmun—dissented.

I would add one final, skeptical note on the matter of the debate over the Establishment Clause. Over the years there were and continue to be innumerable scholarly writings going this way or that way on the wall of separation between church and state. Innumerable, too, have been lawsuits in which this counsel or that invokes it and this judge or that one hands down a decision that goes this way or that way in respect to it. But do these invocations matter?

The first time the Supreme Court quoted Jefferson's letter and its image of a "wall of separation" was in an 1878 decision in a case called *Reynolds* v. *United States*. *Reynolds* involved a Mormon convicted of polygamy. His defense was that polygamy was a tenet of his religion, the Church of Jesus Christ of Latter-Day Saints. The Court invoked the wall of separation, but upheld the conviction. It is safe to assume that the Court would have reached the same conclusion if Jefferson's letter to the Danbury Baptists had been lost in the mail.

The legal system today has not changed since the time of *Reynolds*. Judges write their opinions in terms of legal doctrines and constitutional principles. But what judges decide is not based on any wall of separation even if it is invoked, but upon their view of reality and of justice. Davis provides in this book a readable and insightful account of an important Justice and an important argument, but the importance of the Justice is only partly related to the strengths of his argument.

PREFACE

This is a book about church-state relationships in America. In the firm belief that most of the good literature on this subject is written by specialists for specialists, I have attempted to write something for the nonspecialist who wants to understand more, historically and contemporarily, about this very provocative and controversial subject. This book requires, I believe, by virtue of the complexities inherent in church-state relations as a discipline of study, a sophisticated readership. I have in mind scholars and academicians in fields outside of church-state, government officials, professionals (and not just attorneys), and sophisticated laypersons who do not wish to be crushed under the weight of the historical materials the specialist is of necessity forced to deal with. The specialist has my invitation to read these pages as well; but candidly, while I believe this book not to be devoid of original material, especially in its analysis of the contribution of Chief Justice William H. Rehnquist in the church-state debate, much of the territory covered will be familiar to the church-state scholar.

Most of the modern controversy in the area of church-state relations, not unlike most areas of constitutional law, revolves around the "original intent" of the eighteenth-century framers of the Constitution. We live in a nation where the Constitution is revered, and rightly so, as a binding framework for law and public policy. Unless altered by amendment, every provision of the Constitution is considered to be, in general, a binding precept around which we must shape our legislative and judicial law. This high respect for the Constitution results in heightened controversy over those of its provisions that are vague, or at least over those whose original meanings are now masked by the passage of more than two hundred years of time and debate.

Such is the case with the religion clauses of the First Amendment: "Congress shall make no law respecting the establishment of religion [the Establishment Clause] or prohibiting the free exercise thereof [the Free Exercise Clause]." No respected church-state scholar of today is so bold as to declare, with unqualified conviction, the exact meaning of the religion clauses at the time of their passage. The clauses, standing alone, are too succinct to adequately inform anyone of the plethora of factors that contributed to their wording. The specialist, therefore, must dig deeper by analyzing a wide range of factors, including the history of European church-state patterns, colonial practices, church-state relations in the states after the American Revolution commenced but before the Constitutional Convention convened, the political and religious beliefs (and their intersection) of the delegates to the Constitutional Convention, the question of the virtual absence of the subject of religion in the Constitution and the subsequent outcry in some circles for an amendment protecting religious liberty, the debates of the First Congress which adopted the Bill of Rights, the prevailing church-state patterns of the various states at the time of the First Congress, the debates that took place at the state ratifying conventions, and the understanding of the clauses by the American people at the time of ratification. These matters and more must be mastered before an enlightened opinion, much less a confident conviction, can be formed about the original meaning of the religion clauses.

What I have attempted to do in this volume is to provide a readable but objective summary of the considerable body of facts, people, events, and documents that contributed to the passage of the religion clauses, and then to trace historically the Supreme Court's efforts to properly interpret the framers' intentions. These efforts coalesce to give us a picture of where we are today in terms of American church-state relations.

The methodology I have employed to present these matters is, admittedly, somewhat different from the usual approach, but I trust that it will make this book not only more interesting but also more relevant. I have selected the man who is the pivotal and most important figure in the modern church-state debate, Chief Justice William H. Rehnquist, and have presented the issue of original intent through his eyes (at least as far as his writings will inform us). And for Rehnquist, to be sure, there is no more important consideration in adjudicating church-state controversies than the original intent of the founding fathers. As chief justice of the United States Supreme Court, Rehnquist is in a unique position to guide the Court in new directions, and he is seemingly doing just that. The Court is now on the brink of making sweeping changes in its traditional separationist approaches to the religion clauses.

Is this, then, a book about the original intent of the founding fathers who fashioned the religion clauses, a book about the historical development of church-state relations in America, or a book about Chief Justice Rehnquist? Actually, it is about all of these; and I hope that the reader, in considering these three very interrelated treatments, will gain a better understanding of the fundamental dynamics that shape the direction of church-state relations in America today.

Such a volume is appropriate in light of the present confusion, concern, and controversy over the future direction of the Supreme Court in regard to church-state issues. Because of Rehnquist's position as chief justice, a kind of paranoia exists in some circles about what the future holds for American church-state relations; a kind of euphoria exists in other circles. While neither attitude may be completely justified, these differences in perspective are not surprising. Debate over the permissible level of governmental promulgation, endorsement, and allowance of religious practices in American life is nothing new. What is new is the possibility that the current Court makeup, especially with William Rehnquist as chief justice, portends serious departures from the Court's traditional stances.

I should state without reservation that, for me, the possibility of such serious departures is disturbing. Despite my considerable respect for the impressive judicial abilities of Chief Justice Rehnquist, I find his approach to church-state relations not only difficult to reconcile with what can be determined of the original intent of the framers but also unprotective of fundamental principles of religious liberty.

I intend no personal attack on Chief Justice Rehnquist in these pages, to be sure; my concern is with his views and their possible impact upon American church-state relations. All who study American church-state relations inevitably come down either on the side of separationism (the traditional Supreme Court view) or accommodationism (Rehnquist's view). Though advocates of both views are able to draw substantial historical support for their own positions, I tend to believe, contrary to Chief Justice Rehnquist, that the greater weight of the evidence falls on the side of separationism. Nevertheless, I attempt in these pages to present an objective, fair, and dispassionate treatment of Chief Justice Rehnquist's views and how they may be influential in reshaping church-state relations in America.

To view the debate through the eyes of Chief Justice Rehnquist, it is essential to know something of the man and his judicial philosophy. Thus a brief biographical profile of Rehnquist is given in Chapter 1. For any who desire a fuller treatment of his early life and his educational, legal, and judicial career prior to his appointment to the Supreme Court, Donald E. Boles's excellent book, *Mr. Justice Rehnquist, Judicial Activist*, should be consulted.

Chapter 2 is an overview of the broader Rehnquist judicial philosophy, extending beyond the church-state field. With this background, the reader will be able to better understand how Rehnquist's approach to church-state issues is consistent with his approach to a wide range of constitutional issues.

Chapter 3 attempts to summarize the fundamental importance of original intent in constitutional jurisprudence. Chapter 4 examines the events, people, and documents that around the time of the founding of our nation were instrumental in the adoption of the religion clauses of the First Amendment. Chapter 5 then traces the Supreme Court's efforts in the past two centuries to accurately interpret and apply the religion clauses.

Chapter 6 is an evaluation of Rehnquist's interpretations of the religion clauses, with special emphasis on his understanding of the framers' original intent. Chapter 7 describes the tensions in the present Supreme Court's efforts to formulate a workable framework for applying the religion clauses in church-state controversies.

The two closing chapters, 8 and 9, contain an evaluation of Rehnquist's church-state philosophy, with emphasis upon the controlling aspect of his philosophy—the original intent of the framers—and I also make some observations, in light of Rehnquist's position as chief justice, about possible future directions of the Court in its approach to church-state controversies. My goal, once again, is to enlighten the nonspecialist about church-state matters in America at a time when, because of the philosophical changes in approaches to constitutional interpretation taking place on the Court, greater national attention to these matters is demanded.

I wish to thank Robert T. Miller, Gary Hull, and especially James E. Wood, Jr., all distinguished professors at Baylor University, for their review and critique of this volume. In addition, I wish to thank Donald E. Boles, a political scientist at Iowa State University, and Joan Chandler, an American historian at the University of Texas at Dallas, for their critique and valuable suggestions. The depth of Dr. Wood's grasp of church-state relations was my most valuable critical resource, and his vision for the development of a policy of American church-state relations that is true to history and that best secures religious freedom for all Americans was a source of inspiration to me in the preparation of this book.

I also wish to thank Vicki Novotny, Ruth Ann Taylor, and Beverly Toms, who splendidly performed the task of typing and revising the manuscript, and Kelly Cook, who helped compile the index. Finally, I thank Doris Doyle, surely one of the most delightful editors anyone could hope to work with.

ORIGINAL INTENT

Chapter 1

WILLIAM H. REHNQUIST: A PERSONAL PROFILE

Early Life and Career

William Hubbs Rehnquist was born on 1 October 1924 in Milwaukee, Wisconsin. He and his sister, Jean, were raised in Shorewood, a peaceful, upscale suburb of Milwaukee. His father, William B. Rehnquist, a first-generation American born of Swedish parents, had never attended college and was a wholesale paper salesman. His mother, Margery, was a homemaker and active in civic affairs. She held a degree from the University of Wisconsin and was fluent in five foreign languages.[1]

On graduating from high school, Rehnquist won a scholarship to Kenyon College in Gambier, Ohio. In 1943, after only one semester at Kenyon, he chose to leave school and join the Army Air Corps as a weather observer. North African hostilities had ended by the time he was sent to the stations of Cairo, Casablanca, Tripoli, and Tunis. When he returned from Africa after the war, he was determined not to settle in the frigid climate of his home state of Wisconsin. "I wanted to find someplace like North Africa to go to school," he recalled in a 1985 *New York Times Magazine* interview. He found a suitable place in Palo Alto, California, where he enrolled in Stanford

---

1. John A. Jenkins, "The Partisan: A Talk with Justice Rehnquist," *New York Times Magazine*, 3 March 1985, 31.

University with the benefit of the G.I. Bill federal assistance program. He graduated Phi Beta Kappa with a degree in political science in 1948.[2]

Following graduation, Rehnquist remained at Stanford to receive an M.A. degree in political science. He then ventured to Cambridge, Massachusetts, to earn a second M.A. degree, in government, from Harvard. Deciding upon a career in law, he then returned to Stanford to enter law school, graduating first in his class in 1952.[3] Sandra Day O'Connor, appointed to the Supreme Court in 1981, sometimes dated Rehnquist at Stanford and in 1971, in reflecting upon their law school days, noted that "he quickly rose to the top of the class and, frankly, was head and shoulders above all the rest of us in terms of sheer legal talent and ability."[4] During the 1971 Senate confirmation hearings on Rehnquist's appointment as a Supreme Court justice, a former law school professor recalled: "He was not only the top student in his class but one of the best students in the school over a number of years. He has remained in my mind as one of the most impressive students I have had in some twenty-two years of teaching."[5] Another law school professor added these remembrances:

> As a student he was nothing short of brilliant, dogged in his determination to achieve excellence and persistent in his expectation of excellence on the other side of the podium. I vividly recall that in the give and take of the classroom he tested my stature and

---

2. Quoted portion, ibid.; Hearings Before the Committee on the Judiciary, United States Senate, 92nd Congress, 1st Session on Nominations of William H. Rehnquist, of Arizona, and Lewis F. Powell, Jr., of Virginia, to Be Associate Justices of the Supreme Court of the United States (hereafter cited as 1971 *Nomination Hearings*), 2, 7, 12, 56-57; David L. Shapiro, "William Hubbs Rehnquist" in *The Justices of the United States Supreme Court: Their Lives and Major Opinions*, Leon Friedman, ed. (New York: Chelsea House Publishers, 1978), 5:109; Larry Martz, Ann McDaniel, and Maggie Malone, "A Pair of a Tory Kind," *Newsweek*, 30 June 1986, 20; Lewis J. Lord and Clemens P. Work, "From Lone Dissenter to Chief," *U.S. News and World Report*, 30 June 1986, 18.

3. Martz, McDaniel, and Malone, "A Pair," 20; Lord and Work, "Lone Dissenter," 18; 1971 *Nomination Hearings*, 12.

4. 1971 *Nomination Hearings*, 12.

5. Letter from Phil C. Neal to Senator James O. Eastland (10 November 1971); reprinted in 1971 *Nomination Hearings*, 11.

sharpened my thinking as an instructor many times. He was always forthright and courageous, never equivocal, never evasive, always refined and profound in his analysis of difficult problems; his thoughts were always precisely formulated and precisely expressed.[6]

Following his graduation from Stanford Law School in 1952, Rehnquist accepted an eighteen-month clerkship term under Supreme Court Justice Robert H. Jackson. Others who were clerks during the same period acknowledged considerable respect for his abilities. Several years after completing his clerkship, however, he was criticized by some members of the Court for an article that appeared in the 13 December 1957 issue of *U.S. News and World Report* titled "Who Writes Decisions of the Supreme Court?" in which he faulted several of the justices for giving their clerks too much authority in the writing of Court opinions.[7]

Rehnquist moved to Phoenix, Arizona, in 1953. He married Natalie (Nan) Cornell; they later had three children (James, 1955; Janet, 1957; and Nancy, 1959). In Phoenix, he first became associated with the firm of Evans, Kitchel & Jenckes. He remained in Phoenix for sixteen years as a practicing attorney with four different law firms. The investigation performed by the American Bar Association at the time of Rehnquist's nomination to the Supreme Court in 1971 confirmed that all of his changes to different law firms in Phoenix were made "without hard feelings" and "solely because of Mr. Rehnquist's view that the change would offer him a richer professional experience."[8] As an attorney (specializing mostly in litigation), he won widespread respect among his colleagues for his integrity, diligence, unusual intel-

---

6. Letter from John B. Hurlbut to Senator James O. Eastland (28 October 1971); reprinted in 1971 *Nomination Hearings*, 9.

7. Report of the Standing Committee on the Federal Judiciary of the American Bar Association (2 November 1971); reprinted in 1971 *Nomination Hearings*, 2. Rehnquist had only three other published works prior to his 1971 Supreme Court appointment. They were: "The Arizona Bar Admission Cases: A Strange Judicial Aberration," *American Bar Association Journal* 44 (March 1958): 229-32; "Subdivision Trusts and the Bankruptcy Act," *Arizona Law Review* 3 (Winter 1961): 165-76; and "The Old Order Changeth: The Department of Justice Under John Mitchell," *Arizona Law Review* 12 (Summer 1970): 251-59.

8. Ibid.

lectual abilities, and professional competence. One professional colleague in 1971 remarked, "He is an outstanding lawyer, completely thorough, scholarly, perceptive, articulate, and possessed of the utmost integrity as well as a keen wit."[9]

In February 1969, Rehnquist received an appointment by President Richard Nixon as Assistant Attorney General in the Office of Legal Counsel, United States Department of Justice. As such, he was responsible to the Attorney General for the resolution of most of the legal questions presented to the Department of Justice that did not relate to litigation. In this position he became highly respected among his colleagues. He was one of the most articulate spokesmen, before congressional committees and in public appearances, for the Nixon administration's position on such varied topics as surveillance, wiretapping, obscenity, executive privilege, and the war powers of the president. In 1971, at age 47, Rehnquist was nominated by President Nixon as an associate justice of the Supreme Court of the United States.[10]

1971 Senate Nomination Hearings— A Confirmation of Rehnquist's Conservatism

Despite his outstanding legal record and considerable reputation, Rehnquist's nomination to the Supreme Court in 1971 did not receive uniform approbation. Those who questioned or opposed his nomination were predominantly civil libertarians concerned about his past support of various conservative causes. He had actively participated in the campaign of Barry Goldwater for president in 1964. He had been a vocal critic of the liberal Warren Court. He had urged rejection of a Phoenix city ordinance prohibiting racial discrimination in public accommodations (although once he had seen the legislation's successful impact, he became convinced that his original position was probably wrong). He also opposed portions of the Model State Anti-Discrimi-

---

9. Letter from Jarrel F. Kaplan to Senator Edward W. Brooke (27 October 1971); reprinted in 1971 Nomination Hearings, 8.

10. Report of the Standing Committee on the Federal Judiciary of the American Bar Association (2 November 1971), B2; Shapiro, "William Hubbs Rehnquist," 110.

nation Act while serving as a representative to the National Conference of Commissioners on Uniform State Laws.[11]

During the nomination hearings, Rehnquist was further questioned about a memorandum bearing his initials that was written in 1953 to Justice Jackson while Rehnquist was clerking for Jackson. The memorandum, which related to the issues involved in the Court's consideration of the historic *Brown* v. *Board of Education* case,[12] stated: "I realize that it is an unpopular and unhumanitarian position, for which I have been excoriated by 'liberal' colleagues, but I think *Plessy* v. *Ferguson* [the "separate but equal" decision] was right and should be affirmed. . . ."[13] Rehnquist said it was his recollection that the memorandum had been written to reflect Justice Jackson's views, not his own. Whatever Justice Jackson's views when the memorandum was written, however, he joined a unanimous Court a year later in the *Brown* case in overruling *Plessy*.[14]

Largely because of this record—one highly questionable to the liberal establishment—Rehnquist received a large number of negative confirmation votes (the final vote was 68-26) despite his otherwise seemingly impeccable qualifications. This was in sharp contrast to the 89-1 Senate endorsement of Lewis F. Powell, Jr., who was nominated as an associate justice by President Nixon at the same time Rehnquist was nominated.

The hearings wholly confirmed Rehnquist's political conservatism. Conservative views favoring governmental authority over individual rights were clearly stated in the case of summary arrest procedures, government electronic surveillance, and civil disobedience.[15] Rehnquist clearly implied his assent to a politically conservative stance in an exchange with Senator Charles Mathias of Maryland, which ran as follows:

---

11. Robert E. Riggs and Thomas D. Proffitt, "The Judicial Philosophy of Justice Rehnquist," *Akron Law Review* 16 (Spring 1983): 556-57.

12. 347 U.S. 483 (1954).

13. Quoted in Shapiro, "William Hubbs Rehnquist," 109-10. The *Plessy* case referred to by Rehnquist is at 163 U.S. 537 (1896).

14. Ibid.

15. 1971 *Nomination Hearings*, 43-45 (summary arrests); 139-40 (electronic surveillance); and 166 (civil disobedience).

SENATOR MATHIAS: It has been said here and elsewhere that your political views tend to be conservative. What effect, assuming this is the case, will this have on you as a judge and, consequently, as a man who should be able to decide cases impartially?

MR. REHNQUIST: I would hope none. I realize that that is the same question I would want to be asking a nominee if I were a member of the Senate Judiciary Committee, and I cast about for some way of perhaps giving some evidence of the fact, rather than simply asking you to rely on my assurance.[16]

The hearings also revealed Rehnquist's conservative judicial philosophy, as distinguished from his political philosophy.[17] He commented in the same exchange with Senator Mathias:

I subscribe unreservedly to that philosophy that when you put on the robe, you are not there to enforce your own notions as to what is desirable public policy. You are there to construe as objectively as you possibly can the Constitution of the United States, the statutes of Congress, and whatever relevant legal materials there may be in the case before you.[18]

In describing his own conservative judicial philosophy, Rehnquist repeatedly alluded to the importance of construing the Constitution in light of the framers' original intent as determined from available sources,[19] as opposed to a philosophy that strives to keep the Constitution "in step with the times."[20] This, of course, is a philosophy commonly identified with constitutional judicial conservatism and, since the time of Rehnquist's confirmation as a justice to the Supreme Court in 1971, it has been a guiding principle for Rehnquist in the

---

16. Ibid., 156.

17. Rehnquist did not equate the two. In his testimony, he stated that it was "difficult to pin down the terms 'liberal' and 'conservative,' " and that "they mean something different when one is talking about a political alinement [sic] as opposed to a judicial philosophy of the Supreme Court"; see p. 156 of the 1971 Nomination Hearings.

18. Ibid.

19. For example, ibid., 19, 55, 81-82, 138, and 167.

20. Ibid., 81.

development of his views on church-state issues. In fact, his written opinions in church-state cases since 1971 evidence a confirmed adherence to a narrow interpretation of the framers' intent as expressed in the religion clauses of the First Amendment, and this narrow line of interpretation has consistently served as a basic framework from which he has criticized many of the decisions of the Court on church-state issues.

From Justice to Chief Justice—An Overview

Since his confirmation to the Supreme Court in 1971, William Rehnquist has been widely recognized as one of the brightest and most efficient justices on the Court. In 1986, University of Virginia law professor A. E. Dick Howard observed: "No one on the Court writes with more style, force or assurance. It is hard to match his agility in shaping a record and marshaling arguments to reach a conclusion."[21]

For a decade after his coming onto the Court, the Court's majority seemed unsympathetic to Rehnquist's entreaties from the right. In his 1985 *New York Times Magazine* interview, Rehnquist commented: "I came to the Court sensing, without really having followed it terribly closely, that there were some excesses in terms of constitutional adjudication during the era of the so-called Warren Court. And I felt that I probably would disagree with some of those decisions."[22]

For the decade of the 1970s, Rehnquist seemed perfectly comfortable in disagreeing with many of the Court's decisions. So frequently was he the only dissenter among the justices that his law clerks in 1974 presented him with a small Lone Ranger doll that still sits on the mantel above the fireplace in his chambers. "They referred to me as the lone dissenter," he recalled.[23]

Gradually, however, Rehnquist's keen intellect and insights began to have influence on the Court. By the 1980s, a more conservative

---

21. Quoted in Lewis and Lord, "Lone Dissenter," 18.
22. Jenkins, "The Partisan," 33.
23. Ibid., 34.

Court had begun to emerge. Justices Byron R. White, Lewis F. Powell, Jr. (retired in 1988), Sandra Day O'Connor, and Chief Justice Warren E. Burger often voted with Rehnquist. By 1982, long before the retirement of Chief Justice Burger, Yale law professor Owen Fiss was calling Rehnquist the "leader" of the Court.[24]

Following Chief Justice Burger's retirement in June 1986, President Ronald Reagan nominated Rehnquist as the sixteenth Chief Justice of the Supreme Court. After numerous acrimonious sessions of the Senate confirmation hearings, his nomination was confirmed by the Senate on 17 September 1986. His chief opposition came from civil libertarians in the Senate who stated concerns about "his credibility, his commitment to equality and racial justice, . . . and his commitment to fundamental constitutional values."[25]

Within months after his elevation to chief justice, one Supreme Court staff member reported that Rehnquist had transformed the nation's highest tribunal into a "Happy Court." In addition to possessing notable leadership qualities, Rehnquist is regarded as affable and popular among staff members and other justices. Soon after his appointment, Rehnquist displayed his homespun style by telling his Court colleagues, "Don't call me 'Chief.' I am still Bill."[26]

Rehnquist's unpretentious lifestyle has helped to bring a relaxed atmosphere to the High Court. He drives a Volkswagen Rabbit and often ambles around Court chambers in slacks, desert boots, and a tweed jacket. He is reportedly so efficient in his work that he frequently leaves the Court by 3:00 P.M., often bringing clerks with him to enjoy a game of tennis or croquet.[27] At the time of Rehnquist's nomination as chief justice, Professor A. E. Dick Howard of the University of Virginia Law School wrote:

---

24. Ibid.; Owen Fiss and Charles Krauthammer, "A Return to the Antebellum Constitution: The Rehnquist Court," *New Republic* 185 (10 March 1982): 14.

25. Hearings before the Committee on the Judiciary, United States Senate, 99th Congress (1986), Nominations of William H. Rehnquist (for Chief Justice) and Antonia Scalia (for Associate Justice), 66.

26. Ted Gest, "The Supreme Court With a Smile," *U.S. News and World Report*, 12 January 1987, 23.

27. Ibid.; Martz, McDaniel, and Malone, "A Pair," 20.

No justice of the Court generates more genuine warmth and regard among both his colleagues and others who work at the Court. A former law clerk to Justice White describes Rehnquist as "the nicest person at the Court. Within a few weeks of the Term's commencement, Justice Rehnquist knew all of the clerks by their first names." A justice says of him, "Bill has an exceptional mind. No member of the Court carries more constitutional law in his head than he does." As one looks back over the nearly 15 years Rehnquist has been on the bench, the evidence mounts that he has become one of the most influential members of the Court.[28]

Since joining the Supreme Court in 1971, Rehnquist has been a consistent and profound voice for judicial conservatism. In 1976, Harvard law professor David L. Shapiro published an article that gave a judicial profile of Rehnquist, summarizing a number of his key written opinions and analyzing his general voting patterns.[29] While the article may seem somewhat dated, Shapiro's analysis was accurate at the time and Rehnquist's voting patterns since 1976 have not strayed outside of Shapiro's general conclusions.

Shapiro characterized Rehnquist as "a man of considerable intellectual power" whose judicial product had been adversely affected by "the unyielding character of his ideology."[30] He defined the Rehnquist ideology as embodying the following three propositions:

(1) Conflicts between an individual and the government should, whenever possible, be resolved against the individual.

(2) Conflicts between state and federal authority, whether on an executive, legislative or judicial level, should, whenever possible, be resolved in favor of the states; and

---

28. A. E. Dick Howard, "Justice Rehnquist—A Key Fighter in Major Battles," *American Bar Association Journal* 72 (June 1986), 47.

29. Shapiro, "William Hubbs Rehnquist," 293-357. Shapiro's analysis offered no discussion of Rehnquist's views on church-state matters. It is cited here as a good canvassing of Rehnquist's voting patterns extending to the full array of cases that the Court hears, only a small percentage of which are church-state cases.

30. Ibid., 293.

(3) Questions of the exercise of federal jurisdiction, whether on the district court, appellate court or Supreme Court level, should whenever possible, be resolved against such exercise.[31]

This approach, though quite general, is nonetheless helpful because it reduces Rehnquist's judicial patterns to meaningful categories. Moreover, the propositions represent categories especially derived from an examination of the cases,[32] and thus indicate his judicial philosophy, rather than categories based on political, economic, or social values that people commonly associate with a conservative political philosophy. Clearly, however, as already noted, Rehnquist is a political conservative as well as a judicial conservative.

---

31. Ibid., 294.

32. In Shapiro's words, "A review of *all* the cases in which Justice Rehnquist has taken part indicates that his votes are guided by these three basic propositions." (Emphasis added.) Ibid.

Chapter 2

THE JUDICIAL PHILOSOPHY
OF WILLIAM REHNQUIST

Distinctive Doctrines in Rehnquist's Judicial Philosophy

While this book has as one of its focuses the views of William Rehnquist on church-state issues, and especially the manner in which his understanding of the original intent of the constitutional framers affects his interpretations of the religion clauses, his views in this respect cannot be completely understood apart from a general understanding of certain distinctive doctrines that are a part of his wider judicial philosophy—that is, his judicial philosophy as it extends over the whole spectrum of legal issues that the Supreme Court is called upon to consider. Seen in the context of such broader perspectives, Rehnquist's interpretations and resulting applications of the religion clauses are more easily seen as only one piece of a whole.

A number of exceptional and scholarly works have been written that deal with Rehnquist's judicial philosophy.[1] Despite the rich quality

---

1. Among the best articles are: Thomas Kleven, "The Constitutional Philosophy of Justice William H. Rehnquist," *Vermont Law Review* 8 (Spring 1983): 1-54; Robert E. Riggs and Thomas D. Proffitt, "The Judicial Philosophy of Justice Rehnquist," *Akron Law Review* 16 (Spring 1983): 555-604; John Denvir, "Justice Rehnquist and Constitutional Interpretation," *Hastings Law Journal* 34 (May-July 1983): 1011-53; and Jeff Powell, "The Compleat Jeffersonian: Justice Rehnquist and Federalism," *Yale Law Journal* 91 (1982): 1317-70. All of these articles differ in approach from the Shapiro article discussed in the previous chapter. Shapiro's analysis is of voting pat-

of research and analysis that has been done on Rehnquist's judicial philosophy, however, there is not complete agreement among the commentators on the underlying principles that guide him in deciding cases. This is due in part, no doubt, to the fact that every judicial decision rendered by any Supreme Court justice is the product of an incredibly complex interplay of constitutional construction, political ideology, perceived role of the judiciary, and application of facts. No judge, including Rehnquist, can be neatly assigned to permanent moldings.

Among the commentators who have closely scrutinized his written opinions and voting patterns, however, considerable agreement does emerge concerning certain distinctive doctrines that guide Rehnquist in his decision-making. A selective examination of three of these key distinctives—strict constructionism, judicial deference, and an advocacy of states' rights—will serve well the purpose of this chapter: to understand Rehnquist in a wider judicial context so as to have a general framework for understanding his views on church-state issues.

Strict Constructionism

A common way of analyzing judges relates to methods of construing the Constitution. Judges differ not only as to the meaning of constitutional provisions but also as to the interpretive approaches they employ. There are essentially two models of constitutional interpretation: the strict constructionist and the evolutionist.

The model of strict constructionism argues that "judges deciding constitutional issues should confine themselves to enforcing norms that are stated or clearly implicit in the written Constitution."[2] In modern parlance, this model is referred to as "interpretivism." However, while the name is new, the theory is not. Its roots go back at least to Supreme Court Justice Joseph Story (1811-45), whose for-

---

terns—an examination of what Rehnquist does. The articles cited here seek to analyze *why* Rehnquist votes as he does. The discussion offered here is of the latter variety. An insightful and useful volume, *Rehnquist and the Constitution*, by Sue Davis, was published in 1989 by Princeton University Press and now stands as the best available comprehensive analysis of the Rehnquist judicial philosophy.

2. John Hart Ely, *Democracy and Distrust: A Theory of Judicial Review* (Cambridge, Mass.: Harvard University Press, 1980), 1.

mulation of constitutional interpretation can be clearly seen in the following statement:

> In construing the Constitution of the United States, we are in the first instance to consider, what are its nature and objects, its scope and design, as apparent from the structure of the instrument, viewed as a whole and also viewed in its component parts. Where its words are plain, clear and determinate, they require no interpretation. . . . Where the words admit of two senses, each of which is conformable to general usage, that sense is to be adopted, which without departing from the literal import of the words, best harmonizes with the nature and objects, the scope and design of the instrument.[3]

Professor Ronald Dworkin has suggested that the strict constructionist model is premised on two positive tenets: that law is objectively determinable and that law is logically separate from moral values that are arbitrary or subjective.[4] Dworkin's description is not only succinct but insightful and can readily be discovered in Rehnquist's writings. In Rehnquist's estimation, judges who depart from the constitutional text cease being judges and become, in Rehnquist's words,

> [a] small group of fortunately situated people with a roving commission to second-guess Congress, state legislatures, and state and federal administrative officers concerning what is best for the country. . . .
> Beyond the Constitution and the laws in our society, there simply is no basis other than the individual conscience of the citizen that may serve as a platform for the launching of moral judgments. There is no conceivable way in which I can logically demonstrate to you that the judgments of my conscience are superior to the judgments of your conscience, and vice versa. Many of us necessarily feel strongly and deeply about our own moral judgments, but they remain only personal moral judgments until in some way given the sanction of law.[5]

3. Joseph Story, *Commentaries on the Constitution of the United States*, 3 vols. (Boston: Hilliard, Greay, and Company, 1833), 1:387-88.

4. Ronald Dworkin, *Taking Rights Seriously* (Cambridge, Mass.: Harvard University Press, 1977), 14-22.

5. William H. Rehnquist, "The Notion of a Living Constitution," *Texas Law Review* 54 (May 1976): 693, 704.

In other words, a judge's function is to adhere to the text and abstain from making moral judgments. Such judgments are, according to Rehnquist, better left to the legislator who, while no wiser than the judge, is at least more democratically accountable in a majoritarian-based republic. Such was the rationale for Rehnquist's dissent in *Roe* v. *Wade*.[6] The Court majority enunciated a "right of privacy" arising out of various constitutional amendments that would be applied to the states through the Fourteenth Amendment, but Rehnquist objected on the grounds that such a right "was apparently completely unknown to the drafters of the Amendment . . . the drafters did not intend to have the Fourteenth Amendment withdraw from the States the power to legislate with respect to this matter."[7]

The second model of constitutional interpretation, the evolutionist model, permits changes in the scope of constitutional provisions as contemporary thinking and social conditions shed new light on constitutionally expressed norms. Under strict constructionism, the meaning of the text is fixed and should be adhered to—at least when the intent of the framers is discoverable. Under evolutionism, what was constitutional in one era may become unconstitutional in the next, and vice versa.[8] Evolutionism departs, then, in varying degrees, from the specific intent of the framers, although it may not be totally fair to suggest, as Rehnquist does, that evolutionist decisions are in no way "tied to the language of the Constitution."[9]

Judges who are adherents of evolutionism claim that their decisions are rooted in the Constitution; they claim merely to exercise greater freedom than strict constructionists in expanding the Constitution's underlying principles to meet contemporary needs. Strict constructionism and evolutionism are really opposite ends of the same spectrum. All judges fall somewhere in between the two ends, although most tend to adopt one or the other as a fundamental judicial philosophy. That William Rehnquist favors strict constructionism in constitutional

---

6. 410 U.S. 113 (1973).
7. Ibid., 198, 200.
8. Kleven, "The Constitutional Philosophy of Justice William H. Rehnquist," 3.
9. Rehnquist, "Living Constitution," 698.

interpretation had become axiomatic by the time of his nomination for chief justice in 1986.

Judicial Deference

Another way of analyzing judges relates to modes of judicial review. A deferential judge is one who believes his judicial responsibility is to defer to the judgments of other branches of government. To the extent that a judge is willing to override the judgments of other governmental branches, he or she is an activist. All defer in some cases and override in others, so the issue of deference versus activism is one of degree. Most judges, however, will tend toward an overall philosophy favoring either deference or activism.[10]

Deference reflects a judge's view of the role of the courts in relation to other branches of government. At one extreme, a judge could take the perspective that a court should decide anew the wisdom of every governmental action coming before it. This extreme, however, would be clearly inconsistent with the way in which issues are typically resolved in a democratic society.[11]

By contrast, a judge could go to the opposite extreme and totally defer to all decisions made by other branches of government. That no judge does this in practice demonstrates that all judges to some degree are activists. Various factors might impel a judge toward activism. If, for example, the popular branches of government exceed the limits of their constitutional powers, judges must become, in Rehnquist's words, "the keepers of the covenant."[12] In placing proper limitations upon the other branches of government in keeping with the Constitution, the judge becomes (appropriately, by all accounts) an activist. Or a judge might doubt the justice or wisdom of legislation passed by a political body. Overturning that legislation because it is deemed socially unwise and searching for and discovering constitutional authority on which to ground his or her decision would make a judge (in-

---

10. Kleven, "Constitutional Philosophy," 2.
11. Ibid.
12. Rehnquist, "Living Constitution," 698.

appropriately, by some accounts) an activist.[13]

Of the two examples given above, the second represents the kind of activism in which a judge feels the judiciary has a greater ability to reach correct results than other branches of government. The judge may feel that his or her position of independence, free from the pressures of voter accountability, best facilitates his or her ability to make hard choices that are socially "best." Since even the most activist judge will rely on the Constitution as the source of law for his or her decisions, this activist rationale is similar to Rehnquist's "keepers of the covenant" approach in the first example. However, since it depends more on an affirmative belief in the efficacy of judicial participation in the debate, it is likely to be more interventionist, particularly when the meaning of the Constitution is unclear.[14] It is this type of activism that Rehnquist criticizes as "a formula for an end run around popular government" and "corrosive of the fundamental values of our democratic society."[15]

Rehnquist's dissent in *Furman* v. *Georgia* illustrates his adherence to the principle of judicial deference to decisions of state governments.[16] Reacting to the Court majority's decision to invalidate the Georgia death penalty as cruel and unusual punishment, Rehnquist protested: "The Court's judgments today strike down a penalty that our nation's legislators have thought necessary since our country was founded."[17] While admitting that "overreaching the legislative and executive branches may result in the sacrifice of individual protections that the Constitution was designed to secure against action of the State," he insisted that the "judicial overreaching" evident in the decision sacrificed "the equally important right of the people to govern themselves."[18]

The same deference theme was expressed by Rehnquist in his dissent from a five-to-four decision in *Trimble* v. *Gordon*,[19] which invalidated an Illinois law prohibiting intestate inheritance by illegitimate children from their fathers. Rehnquist reasoned that policy decisions are to be

---

13. Kleven, "Constitutional Philosophy," 2-3.
14. Kleven, "Constitutional Philosophy," 6-7.
15. Rehnquist, "Living Constitution," 705.
16. 408 U.S. 238 (1972).
17. Ibid., 465.
18. Ibid., 470.
19. 430 U.S. 762 (1977).

made by the people through their elected representatives, and not by judges. He added that the "Constitutional Convention in 1787 rejected the idea that members of the federal judiciary should sit on a council of revision and veto laws which it considered unwise"[20] and that the "Civil War Amendments did nothing to alter that decision."[21]

An Advocacy of States' Rights

Much of this nation's political history is the story of the American struggle to define the relationship between the states and the federal government. Prior to the adoption of the Constitution, the Union operated as a loose confederation of states in which "each state retain[ed] its sovereignty, freedom, and independence."[22] The Constitution was born out of a perceived need to vest the federal government with expanded powers, especially in the realms of defense, commerce, and taxation. Yet the concern among the various states about releasing too much power to the federal government resulted in the ratification of the Tenth Amendment (1791), which provides for the retention by the states of powers not delegated to the national government.[23] The meaning of federalism (the division of power between state and national government) has been the subject of vigorous political debate ever since. In recent history, the Reagan administration, citing the modern wave of virtually plenary federal power, frequently stressed the need to reestablish the doctrine of state sovereignty. The Bush administration is equally committed to state sovereignty, but has been less vocal in its promotion.

William Rehnquist is a strong proponent of state sovereignty and the limitation of congressional power in regard to states' rights. In *Trimble* v. *Gordon*,[24] Rehnquist argued that

---

20. Ibid., 778.
21. Ibid.
22. *Articles of Confederation*, Article II.
23. The Tenth Amendment provides: "The powers not delegated to the United States by the Constitution, nor prohibited by it to the States, are reserved to the States respectively, or to the people."
24. 430 U.S. 762 (1977).

the Framers of the Constitution adopted a system of checks and balances conveniently lumped under the descriptive head of "federalism," whereby all power was originally presumed to reside in the people of the States who adopted the Constitution. The Constitution delegated some authority to the federal executive, some to the federal legislature, some to the federal judiciary, and reserved the remaining authority normally associated with sovereignty to the States and to the people in the States.[25]

Rehnquist's majority opinion in *National League of Cities* v. *Usery*[26] has been described by one writer as the centerpiece of Rehnquist's theory of federalism.[27] In *Usery*, the Court held that Congress could not require state or local governments to pay the minimum wages applicable to individuals. Rehnquist wrote that the structure of the Constitution withheld from Congress any power to regulate the operating of "states as states."[28] The case was significant because it reintroduced into the Court's jurisprudence the long-absent doctrine of state sovereignty and discredited the conventional wisdom that there were virtually no enforceable judicial limits on congressional power. The *Usery* case has not been followed in later Supreme Court cases,[29] but it remains central to Rehnquist's constitutional jurisprudence.

Rehnquist's belief that states have the right to have their laws function without federal interference in the areas reserved to them is minimally influenced by the Civil War Amendments. In his dissent in *Trimble*, he contended that although the Civil War Amendments "sharply altered the balance of power between the Federal and State Governments," they did so only in specific, historically identifiable ways and were not to be construed to affect radically "the original understanding at Philadelphia."[30] It is not surprising, then, that Rehn-

---

25. Ibid., 777-78.

26. 426 U.S. 833 (1976). As explained in the next chapter, *Usery* was later overruled in *Garcia* v. *San Antonio Metropolitan Transit Authority*, 105 S. Ct. 1005 (1985).

27. Powell, "The Compleat Jeffersonian," 1325.

28. 426 U.S. 833 (1976), 845.

29. Invocations of Tenth Amendment, *Usery*-like arguments have failed, for example, in *Hodel* v. *Indiana*, 452 U.S. 314 (1981), and *Hodel* v. *Virginia Surface Mining & Reclamation Association*, 452 U.S. 264 (1981).

30. 430 U.S. 762 (1977), 778.

quist seeks to limit the Fourteenth Amendment in order to minimize the states' vulnerability to federal encroachments. This is a special problem for Rehnquist because the Amendment on its face purports to expand the power of the federal government and limit the power of the states. Rehnquist concedes that the structure of federalism was altered somewhat by the Civil War Amendments, but insists that the Amendments

> were not designed to accomplish this purpose [the alteration of the balance of power between federal and state governments] in some vague way which was ultimately to be discovered by this Court more than a century after their enactment. Their language contained the mechanisms by which their purpose was to be accomplished. Congress might affirmatively legislate under Section 5 of the Fourteenth Amendment, and the courts could strike down state laws found directly to violate the dictates of the Amendments.
>
> This was strong medicine, and it intended to be such. But it cannot be read apart from the general understanding at Philadelphia. . . .[31]

In order to preserve the "original understanding at Philadelphia," Rehnquist has creatively employed a number of judicial devices that minimize the impact of the Civil War Amendments.[32] Of particular note in the present connection is Rehnquist's systematic rejection of the Court's doctrine of selective incorporation first adopted in *Gitlow* v. *New York*.[33]

Rehnquist's criticism of the incorporation doctrine is without diffidence. He has referred to the doctrine as "the mysterious process of transmogrification by which [a guarantee of the Bill of Rights] was held to be 'incorporated' and made applicable to the States by the Fourteenth Amendment."[34] He has labeled incorporation as a "judicial building block" used by the Court to construct constitutional doctrine

---

31. Ibid.

32. A good discussion of several of such judicial devices is presented in the Powell article previously cited, "The Compleat Jeffersonian: William Rehnquist and Federalism"; see n. 21. Such devices, other than Rehnquist's rejection of the incorporation doctrine, are beyond the scope of this study.

33. 268 U.S. 652 (1925).

34. *Carter* v. *Kentucky*, 450 U.S. 288 (1981).

with an "increasingly remote" and even "incomprehensible" connection to the Constitution text.[35]

With regard to the First Amendment, Rehnquist has been willing to approve of its incorporation into the Fourteenth Amendment only in a limited sense. In *Buckley* v. *Valeo*,[36] Rehnquist stated:

> I am of the opinion that not all of the strictures which the First Amendment imposes upon Congress are carried over against the States by the Fourteenth Amendment, but rather that it is only the "general principle" of free speech, that the latter incorporates.
>
> Given this view, cases which deal with state restrictions on First Amendment freedoms are not fungible with those which deal with restrictions imposed by the Federal Government. . . .[37]

That Rehnquist is willing to make applicable to the states by incorporation only First Amendment free speech freedoms has remarkable impact on his church-state views. The religion clauses of the First Amendment have each been selectively incorporated by the Court into the Fourteenth Amendment (the Establishment Clause in *Everson* v. *Board of Education*[38] and the Free Exercise Clause in *Cantwell* v. *Connecticut*[39]) and, accordingly, restrict the freedom of states from enacting "establishment of religion" legislation and from denying religious "free exercise" rights. This might not be totally objectionable to Rehnquist but for the High Court's interpretations of the religion clauses that are more expansive than he is willing to permit. The implications of the Court's historic interpretations of the religion clauses in relation to Rehnquist's own interpretations will be explored in detail in subsequent chapters.

---

35. *Snead* v. *Stringer*, 102 S.Ct. 535 (1981), 536, n. 1.
36. 424 U.S. 1 (1976).
37. Ibid., 291.
38. 330 U.S. 1 (1947).
39. 310 U.S. 296 (1940).

The Distinctive Doctrines of Rehnquist's Judicial Philosophy in Perspective

The interpretative principles employed by Rehnquist just discussed—strict constructionism, deference, and an advocacy of states' rights—are considerably interrelated. In many of Rehnquist's written opinions, all three principles surface simultaneously. The *Usery* case, discussed above as an illustration of Rehnquist's commitment to states' rights, is a good example. There, the Court held that state and local government employees were not subject to federal minimum-wage laws. Writing for a five-to-four Court majority, Rehnquist emphasized the need for the Court to respect the Tenth Amendment (strict constructionism); he stressed the right of states to enjoy a "separate and independent existence" free from congressional interference (deference);[40] and he asserted that "this Court has never doubted" the existence of state sovereignty limitations on congressional power (federalism of states' rights).[41]

The theme of these interrelated principles is simply this: federal interference with state activities is to be judicially disfavored because that was the intent of the constitutional framers.[42] In Rehnquist's view, the judiciary must recognize

> the understanding of those who drafted and ratified the Constitution that the States were sovereign in many respects, and that although their legislative authority could be superseded by Congress in many areas where Congress was competent to act, Congress was nonetheless not free to deal with a State as if it were just another individual or business enterprise subject to regulation.[43]

---

40. 426 U.S. 833 (1976), 846.

41. Ibid., 857.

42. This emphasis on the protection of states' rights against federal power is the principal justification for a number of commentators in their characterization of Rehnquist as a judicial activist. Powell (note 30) and Fiss and Krauthammer (note 24) are notable examples. Also, Donald Boles, in his first of a proposed three-book series about Justice Rehnquist, draws on the same "activist" theme, suggested most prominently in the title to his book, *Mr. Justice Rehnquist, Judicial Activist* (Ames, Iowa: University of Iowa Press, 1987).

43. *Fry v. United States,* 421 U.S. 542 (1975), 557.

What is the source of Rehnquist's strong emphasis on states' rights? His claim is that history "too well known to warrant more than brief mention"[44] demonstrates the congruence of his states' rights theory with the intent of the framers and excludes alternative interpretations. On initial consideration, Rehnquist's historical claim seems familiar and supportable. State sovereignty and limited federal government are certainly authentic expressions of a central strand of American constitutional philosophy. It is a philosophy that found its classic expression in the thought of Thomas Jefferson. It is Jeffersonian republicanism, says legal scholar Jeff Powell, that is the best source and description of Rehnquist's emphasis on states' rights.[45] Powell's connection of Rehnquist to Jeffersonian thought is intriguing as well as plausible, and worthy of closer scrutiny.

Jefferson considered that the simple economic life of his day necessitated little regulation and that the welfare of the people could best be secured through the state and local units of government, which would naturally understand the needs of each community better than a more distant government. He advocated a national government of sufficient strength and prestige to control commercial and diplomatic relations with foreign countries, but in domestic affairs he believed that federal authority should be confined strictly to those powers enumerated in the Constitution and that other matters should be left to the states and to individuals.[46]

For much of the period from 1789 to 1861 there persisted a basic clash between the political leaders who upheld the Hamilton-Marshall-Federalist conception of a strong nationalist government, and those who insisted with Jefferson that the Constitution provided for a federal government of limited delegated authority with the residue of powers left to the states and to the citizens.[47] In the Jeffersonian tradition, the transcendent goal of freedom is unattainable unless the national government is kept as small and unobtrusive as possible.[48]

---

44. *Trimble* v. *Gordon*, 430 U.S. 762 (1977), 777.

45. Powell, "The Compleat Jeffersonian," 1363.

46. Alfred H. Kelly and Winfred A. Harbison, *The American Constitution: Its Origins and Development*, 3rd ed. (New York: W. W. Norton, 1963), 205.

47. Ibid., 203.

48. Powell, "The Compleat Jeffersonian," 1364.

"This vision of limited government has haunted our history from its beginning," says Powell, "and is reflected frequently . . . in the opinions of Justice Rehnquist."[49] Jefferson is so thoroughly identified with the ideal of liberty, continues Powell, that even the patron saint of strong national government, Abraham Lincoln, found it necessary to invoke Jefferson and his ennobled ideals, stating that "the principles of Jefferson are the definitions and axioms of a free society."[50] It is this almost sanctified tradition in American intellectual history, says Powell, that Rehnquist's constitutional theory taps, and that gives his federalism such appeal.[51]

Rehnquist frequently writes that the protection of states' rights was paramount to the framers. If there is a problem with Rehnquist's theory, it is in the historical accuracy of such a claim. To be sure, the idea of state sovereignty was the subject of heated debate during the campaign for ratification of the Constitution. Unlike the Articles of Confederation, the Constitution contained no guarantee of absolute state sovereignty. The opponents of the Constitution, the anti-federalists, claimed that it destroyed state sovereignty altogether.[52] Arguing against ratification in the Virginia convention of June 1788, Patrick Henry attacked the proposed Constitution as an attempt to replace the old, loosely knit confederation with "a great consolidated government."[53] Henry added, "It will destroy the state governments and swallow the liberties of the people, without giving previous notice."[54]

The Federalist response to these charges was an active campaign to convince the Constitution's opponents that the new government would not destroy the sovereignty of the states or become an instrument of tyranny. Alexander Hamilton, James Madison, and John Jay led this effort by producing The Federalist Papers, a series of eighty-five articles designed to explain the benefits of the new Constitution, and

---

49. Ibid.
50. Letter from Abraham Lincoln to Committee of Boston Republicans (16 April 1859), quoted in Powell, "The Compleat Jeffersonian," 1364.
51. Ibid.
52. Powell, "The Compleat Jeffersonian," 1365-68.
53. Patrick Henry, Address to Virginia Ratifying Convention (June 1788), quoted in Powell, "The Compleat Jeffersonian," 1366.
54. Ibid., 1367.

especially why the consolidation of the states into a "Union" was best for the American people.[55]

Eventually, the Federalist effort to win ratification of the Constitution was successful. In the spirit of compromise and unity, the Constitution was ratified in 1789. In time, the Constitution became sacrosanct, but disagreement as to the true meaning of the document has never ceased.[56] The notion, however, that there was a clear-cut "intent" of the framers is suspect, if not a fiction. Absolute state sovereignty, clearly, was never intended by the Federalist sentiment.[57]

Powell proposes that Rehnquist's federalism lies squarely within the tradition of Jeffersonian republicanism. Accordingly, he says, Rehnquist (with Jefferson) assumes that freedom means local political autonomy. Powell then lists a number of other conclusions in which Rehnquist and Jefferson would concur:

> They [Rehnquist and Jefferson] conclude from this that the chief threat to freedom comes from a powerful central government. They assume that the state governments, being closer to the people, will be both competent and willing to guarantee the political and civil rights of their citizens. . . . Therefore, the Constitution is to be construed to limit severely the federal government's sphere of authority and thus reserve for the state governments . . . autonomous control over most domestic concerns.[58]

In order to fit the Civil War Amendments into this minimal federal scheme, says Powell, "Rehnquist views them as a mere perfection of the Jeffersonian axiom that all citizens should possess equal rights vis-à-vis the government."[59]

Rehnquist's conviction that the intentions of the framers is an objective basis for the constitutional law must be questioned at the point of its historical veracity, argues Powell. The evidence that the framers intended an alliance of sovereign state governments dedicated

---

55. Kelly and Harbison, *The American Constitution*, 151-55.
56. Ibid., 156-64.
57. Powell, "The Compleat Jeffersonian," 1363-70.
58. Ibid., 1365.
59. Ibid., 1365-66.

to the preservation of their local autonomy is challenged, he says, if not superseded, by evidence that the framers intended to establish a vigorous national government for the purpose of securing the liberties of the sovereign people. Powell concludes by stating that Rehnquist's attempt to use the intention of the framers as an objective basis for constitutional law fails at its most fundamental and crucial point— its connection to history.[60]

Whether or not one accepts the totality of Powell's thesis of a link between Rehnquist and Jeffersonian thought,[61] it is clear that Rehnquist's reliance upon states' rights, grounded in the intent of the framers, is the foundation for his constitutional jurisprudence. The implications of this theme extend even to cases involving the First Amendment religion clauses. Rehnquist's understanding of the original intent of the framers in the drafting of the religion clauses, with emphasis upon his stated belief that the states were to remain sovereign over the matter of religion, shapes his own interpretations of the religion clauses.

60. Ibid., 1369.

61. Powell's thesis is supported by Owen Fiss and Charles Krauthammer, "The Rehnquist Court," 20.

Chapter 3

THE CONTEMPORARY DEBATE OVER THE ORIGINAL INTENT OF THE FRAMERS

The Abiding Constitution

William Gladstone, the great British statesman and prime minister, once described the American Constitution as "the most wonderful work ever struck off at a given time by the brain and purpose of man."[1] Americans cannot but be pleased by this tribute, and it is accepted by most as being largely true. Certainly the Constitution has withstood the most decisive of all tests—that of time. The hallowed document drafted by fifty-five delegates to the Constitutional Convention in 1787 is now the oldest written constitution in the world. Drafted for an eighteenth-century republic of fewer than four million people, the Constitution survived the transition from an agrarian society to an industrial one and is now surviving the transition from an industrial society to a technological one. That the Constitution still provides a stable base for American society is indeed an abiding testimonial to its extraordinary character.

In light of these facts, it is natural to uphold the Constitution's framers as men of remarkable wisdom and foresight. Throughout this nation's history, the purposes and intentions of the founding fathers

---

1. Quoted in Alfred H. Kelly and Winfred A. Harbison, *The American Constitution*, 1.

have usually been considered relevant in construing and applying the Constitution's provisions. Under most contemporary theories of constitutional interpretation, the intentions of the framers continue to be considered relevant, albeit in varying degrees.

This chapter and the next examine the issue of the original intent of the constitutional framers from various perspectives—political, philosophical, historical, and judicial. The Supreme Court is, ultimately, the arbiter of how relevant and binding the intentions of the framers are in constitutional interpretation. Accordingly, after considering in this chapter a number of important perspectives on the broad issue of "original intent" as a guideline to constitutional interpretation in general, the next chapter narrows to a consideration of original intent as a guideline to interpretation of the First Amendment religion clauses and then the following chapter (Chapter 5) provides a review of significant Supreme Court decisions that reveal the Court's level of commitment to the original intentions of the founding fathers.

Attorney General Meese's Jurisprudence of Original Intention

Perhaps never in this nation's history has a particular doctrine of constitutional interpretation been advanced as so major a theme by the executive branch of government as during the administration of President Ronald Reagan. The administration's chief spokesman in the effort was Attorney General Edwin Meese III. Meese dramatically stepped up the Reagan administration's push for what he called a "jurisprudence of original intention"[2] in a series of speeches delivered in 1985.

The Meese speeches are worthy of a brief examination for two reasons. First, even though the Bush administration subsequently has been virtually silent on reviving the "true intentions" of the framers

---

2. Address by Attorney General Edwin Meese to the American Bar Association, "The Supreme Court of the United States: Bulwark of a Limited Constitution," Washington D.C., 9 July 1985; reprinted in *South Texas Law Review* 27 (1986): 455-66. (Hereafter called Meese Speech).

(presumably because of the backlash of criticism directed at Meese), the speeches are instructive as the latest example in a historical chain of efforts to resurrect the elusive "original intent" of the framers. Second, despite the departure of Meese from the public limelight and the passing of the Reagan years, the call for a "jurisprudence of original intention" is still a vibrant movement among many political conservatives in the decade of the nineties.

The first Meese speech was given at the annual meeting of the American Bar Association in Washington, D.C., on 9 July 1985. That speech was followed by subsequent addresses on the same topic presented again to the American Bar Association on 17 July 1985 and to the District of Columbia Chapter of the Federalist Society Lawyers Division at Georgetown University on 15 November 1985.[3] Because the first speech contained the essential elements of all three of Meese's messages, it is the only one that will be discussed here.

Meese expressed in his speech his view of the purpose of the Constitution: "the creation of limited but also energetic government, institutions with the power to govern, but also with structures to keep the power in check."[4] A primary constitutional structure to keep the power in check, according to Meese, is the judiciary:

> The intended role of the judiciary generally, and the Supreme Court in particular, was to serve as the "bulwark of a limited constitution." The Founders believed that judges would not fail to regard the Constitution as fundamental law and would regulate their decisions by it. As the "faithful guardians of the Constitution," the judges were expected to resist any political effort to depart from the literal provisions of the Constitution. The standard of interpretation applied by the judiciary must focus on the text and the drafters' original intent.[5]

---

3. Jonathan K. Van Patten, "The Partisan Battle Over the Constitution: Meese's Jurisprudence of Original Intention and Brennan's Theory of Contemporary Ratification," *Marquette Law Review* 70 (Spring 1987): 391-92.

4. Meese Speech, 457.

5. Ibid., 469-70; quoted portions are from Alexander Hamilton's *The Federalist*, No. 78.

However, Meese continued, the federal courts, and especially the Supreme Court, have lost sight of upholding the central purpose of the Constitution, namely, to limit the power of the federal government. He then proceeded to comment on the Supreme Court's decisions during the 1984 term in three judicial areas, accusing the Court of having a propensity to "roam at large in a veritable constitutional forest."[6] The three areas that he covered were: federalism, criminal law, and freedom of religion.

Federalism

Meese expressed his dismay at the Court's decision in *Garcia* v. *San Antonio Metropolitan Transit Authority*,[7] which denied that the Tenth Amendment protects states from federal laws regulating the wages and hours of state or local employees. There the Court overruled *National League of Cities* v. *Usery*,[8] the "centerpiece" of William Rehnquist's theory of federalism.[9] Meese affirmed that federalism was one of the most basic principles of the Constitution. He added, "By allowing the states sufficient sovereignty to govern, we better secure our ultimate goal of political liberty through decentralized government."[10]

Criminal Law

Meese was complimentary of the Court for taking a more "progressive stance" on Fourth Amendment cases, specifically for permitting "warrantless searches under certain limited circumstances."[11] The Court's decisions, he stated, helped repair "some of the damage previously done through its piecemeal incorporation through the fourteenth amendment."[12]

---

6. Ibid., 458.
7. 105 S. Ct. 1005 (1985).
8. 426 U.S. 833 (1976).
9. Powell, "The Compleat Jeffersonian," 1325.
10. Meese Speech, 459.
11. Ibid., 460.
12. Ibid.

Freedom of Religion

Meese briefly reviewed four Establishment Clause cases,[13] the results of which he deemed would have been considered "bizarre" by the "founding generation."[14] The purpose of the First Amendment, stated Meese, "was to prohibit religious tyranny, not to undermine religion generally."[15] He argued that the purpose of the Establishment Clause was never to require a "strict neutrality between religion and non-religion."[16] Instead, Meese added, "the establishment clause of the first amendment was designed to prohibit Congress from establishing a national church. The belief was that the Constitution should not allow Congress to designate a particular faith or sect as politically above the rest."[17]

Meese blamed the incorporation doctrine, which rests upon an "intellectually shaky foundation," as the cause of the "tangled case law" in the area of religious freedom.[18] He reminded his audience that the Bill of Rights was not applied to the states in any respect until 1925,[19] and suggested that "nowhere else has the principle of

---

13. The cases were *Grand Rapids School District* v. *Ball*, 105 S. Ct. 3216 (1985), which disallowed shared time and community education programs offered in space leased from parochial schools; *Aguilar* v. *Felton*, 105 S. Ct. 3232 (1985), which invalidated a public-assisted program of secular instruction for low-income students in sectarian schools; *Wallace* v. *Jaffree*, 105 S. Ct. 2479 (1985), which struck down an Alabama statute calling for a moment of silence for meditation or voluntary prayer because it had as its sole purpose the fostering of religious activity in the public schools; and *Thornton* v. *Caldor*, 105 S. Ct. 2914 (1985), in which the Court struck down a Connecticut law prohibiting private employers from discharging employees for refusing to work on their sabbath, reasoning that the law had the primary effect of advancing religion because the law effectively made the sabbath concerns of workers dominant over all secular concerns at the workplace.

14. Meese Speech, 464.

15. Ibid.

16. Ibid.

17. Ibid.

18. Ibid., 462-63.

19. The Bill of Rights was first applied in *Gitlow* v. *New York*, 268 U.S. 652 (1925), 666: "For present purposes we may and do assume that freedom of speech and of the press—which are protected by the First Amendment from abridgment by Congress—are among the fundamental personal rights and 'liberties' protected by the due process clause of the Fourteenth Amendment from impairment by the States." The Establishment Clause was first applied to the states in *Everson* v. *Board of Education*, 330 U.S. 1 (1947).

Federalism been dealt such a politically violent and constitutionally suspect blow as by the theory of incorporation."[20]

The Attorney General had words of praise, however, for Justice Rehnquist's dissent in *Wallace* v. *Jaffree*.[21] In that case, a six-to-three majority had struck down an Alabama statute calling for a moment of silence for "meditation or voluntary prayer" because the legislative history of the statute indicated that its sole purpose was the fostering of religious activity in public school classrooms. Rehnquist, in the longest dissent he had offered in his fourteen-year Supreme Court tenure, called for a reassessment of the Court's entire approach to the Establishment Clause: "If a constitutional theory has no basis in the history of the amendment it seeks to interpret, is difficult to apply, and yields unprincipled results, I see little use in it."[22] Rehnquist went on to state that in his view the purpose of the Establishment Clause was to prevent the designation of a national church and to prevent the federal government from "asserting a preference for one religious denomination or sect over others."[23] Meese asserted his agreement with Rehnquist's views.

The Reaction to the Meese Call
for a Jurisprudence of Original Intention

Reaction to the Meese emphases was swift and thunderous. Editorials, letters to the editor, and academic criticism appeared instantly. In addition, at least four federal judges, including two Supreme Court justices, quickly responded to the Meese attack on the federal judiciary's

---

20. Meese Speech, 463-64. On 17 October 1985, Meese clarified his position on the incorporation doctrine. He stated that he was not calling for a revocation of the doctrinal developments since *Gitlow* because "precedent, stability, and predictability are important. [I do not] think it would be either prudent or necessary to roll back the clock"; quoted in Howard Ball, "The Convergence of Constitutional Law and Politics in the Reagan Administration: The Exhumation of the 'Jurisprudence of Original Intention' Doctrine," *Cumberland Law Review* 17 (Summer 1987): 880.

21. 105 S. Ct. 2479 (1985).

22. Ibid., 2519 (Rehnquist, J., dissenting).

23. Ibid., 2520 (Rehnquist, J., dissenting).

methodology. Such a response was remarkable because, traditionally, federal judges remain above the political debates that necessarily accompany the legal issues with which they deal.[24]

Abner Mikva, a judge of the United States Court of Appeals of the District of Columbia Circuit, termed Meese's remarks an attack on "settled and sensible law."[25] Irving R. Kaufman, presiding judge for the United States Court of Appeals, Second Circuit, remarked that as a federal judge he often found it impossible to "ascertain the 'intent of the framers,' and even more problematic to try to dispose of a constitutional question by giving great weight to the intent argument."[26] Kaufman stated that "even if it were possible to decide hard cases on the basis of original intent or originalism, that methodology would conflict with a judge's duty to apply the Constitution's underlying principles to changing circumstances."[27]

Supreme Court justices William J. Brennan and John P. Stevens also took the opportunity to speak out publicly in response to Meese's remarks. In a speech to Georgetown University's College of Law, Brennan had harsh words for the advocates of "original intent":

> There are those who find legitimacy in fidelity to what they call "the original intentions of the Framers." In its most doctrinaire incarnation, this view demands that Justices discern exactly what the Framers thought about the question under consideration and simply follow that intention in resolving the case before them. It is a view that feigns self-effacing deference to the specific judgments of those who forged our original social compact. But in truth it is little more than arrogance cloaked in humility. It is arrogant to pretend that from our vantage we can gauge accurately the intent of the Framers on application of principle to specific, contemporary questions.[28]

---

24. Ball, "The Convergence of Constitutional Law," 880-81.

25. Quoted in ibid., 877.

26. Irving R. Kaufman, "What Did the Founding Fathers Intend?" *New York Times Magazine*, 23 February 1986, 42.

27. Ibid.

28. Address by Justice William J. Brennan, Jr., "The Constitution of the United States: Contemporary Ratification," Georgetown University, 12 October 1985; reprinted in *South Texas Law Review* 27 (1986): 433-55.

For Brennan, who retired from the Court in 1990, a jurisprudence of original intention would "turn a blind eye to social progress and eschews adaptation of overarching principles to changes of social circumstance."[29] The justice referred to one of federalism's principal claims: that "because ours is a government of the people's elected representatives, substantive value choices should by and large be left to them."[30] Brennan struck hard at such a claim with the following rebuff:

> The view that all matters of substantive policy should be resolved through the majoritarian process . . . ultimately will not do. Unabashed enshrinement of majoritarianism would permit the imposition of a social caste system or wholesale confiscation of property so long as approved by a majority of the fairly elected, authorized legislative body. Our Constitution could not abide such a situation. It is the very purpose of our Constitution—and particularly of the Bill of Rights—to declare certain values transcendent, beyond the reach of temporary political majorities.[31]

Given these points, Brennan added, the federal judiciary has to "read the Constitution in the only way that we can: as twentieth-century Americans. We look to the history of the time of framing and to the intervening history of interpretation."[32]

Later that fall, in a speech to the Federal Bar Association in Chicago on 24 October 1985, Supreme Court Justice John P. Stevens added his own response to some of Meese's remarks of 9 July 1985. "The development of his argument is somewhat incomplete," said Stevens, "because its concentration on the original intentions of the Framers of the Bill of Rights overlooks the . . . profound importance of the Civil War and the post-war amendments on the structure of our government. . . ."[33] Stevens emphasized that the Civil War Amendments

---

29. Ibid., 436.
30. Ibid.
31. Ibid.
32. Ibid., 438.
33. Address by Justice John P. Stevens, "The Supreme Court of the United States: Reflections After a Summer Recess," Chicago, 24 October 1985; reprinted in *South Texas Law Review* 27 (1986): 451-52. (Hereafter called Stevens Speech.)

altered significantly the relationship between the federal government and the states, and that no Supreme Court justice "during the past sixty years has questioned [incorporation]."[34] Stevens, for whatever reasons, declined to comment on Justice Rehnquist's revealed doubts about the soundness of the incorporation doctrine.[35]

Stevens did express his disagreement, however, with Meese's endorsement of Justice Rehnquist's dissenting opinion in *Wallace* v. *Jaffree*—that the Establishment Clause was originally designed to guarantee strict neutrality among Christian sects but did not contemplate strict neutrality between religion and nonreligion. Stevens noted that he was "not at all sure that men like James Madison, Thomas Jefferson, Benjamin Franklin, or the pamphleteer, Thomas Paine, would have regarded strict neutrality on the part of government between religion and non-religion as 'bizarre.' "[36] He characterized the "founding generation" as a "broad and diverse" classification, saying in effect that the original intent of the framers regarding the Establishment Clause is uncertain.[37]

Original Intention as a Proper Form of Inquiry

The Meese-Brennan/Stevens debate over a "jurisprudence of original intention" is but a microcosmic perspective on a debate that today engages participants in many settings—law schools, think tanks, judicial conferences, and political gatherings. The debate raises the fundamental question of the extent to which it is proper to invoke history ("the original understanding at Philadelphia")[38] as a normative guide to the meaning of the Constitution.

Raoul Berger has stated that the "current indifference to the 'original intention' . . . is a relatively recent phenomenon."[39] The Constitution,

---

34. Ibid., 452.

35. See, for example, *Trimble* v. *Gordon*, 430 U.S. 762 (1977) (Rehnquist, J., dissenting).

36. Stevens Speech, 453.

37. Ibid., 452-53.

38. *Trimble* v. *Gordon*, 430 U.S. 762 (1977), 778 (Rehnquist, J., dissenting).

39. Raoul Berger, *Government by Judiciary* (Cambridge, Mass.: Harvard University Press, 1977), 363.

he says, "was written against a background of interpretive presuppositions"—chiefly, that the goal of future interpreters would be to carry out the framers' intent.[40] As a consequence, Berger contends, the intentions of the framers should control constitutional interpretation, because it is only by examining their "original intent" that the interpreter can discover the normative meaning of the Constitution. If Berger is correct, it is imperative to know the "original intent" of the framers. It becomes especially important to know the "original intent" of the framers in their drafting of the religion clauses, because in the words of former Justice Wiley Rutledge, "No provision of the Constitution is more closely tied to or given content by its generating history than the religious clause[s] of the First Amendment."[41]

Conversely, some scholars have argued that the framers' intentions are irrelevant to the task of establishing constitutional norms. Terrance Sandalow, for example, has argued that historical evidence of the framers' intent cannot constrain modern interpretation.[42] Michael Perry has admitted a theoretical legitimacy of judicial enforcement of the framers' intentions, but suggests that in practice modern constitutional lawmaking need not depend on historical argument.[43]

Did the framers' themselves see binding character in their intentions? That is, we might ask not what later interpreters have actually done in construing the Constitution, but what the framers themselves said others should do. An initial inquiry might be made of the "Father of the Constitution," James Madison. Madison propounded:

> I entirely concur in the propriety of resorting to the sense in which the Constitution was accepted and ratified by the nation. In that sense alone it is the legitimate Constitution. And if that be not the guide in expounding it, there can be no security for a consistent and stable, more than for a faithful, exercise of its powers.[44]

---

40. Ibid., 365-66.

41. *Everson v. Board of Education*, 330 U.S. 1 (1947), 33 (Rutledge, J., dissenting).

42. Terrance Sandalow, "Constitutional Interpretation," *Michigan Law Review* 79 (April 1981): 1033.

43. Michael Perry, *The Constitution, the Courts, and Human Rights* (New Haven, Conn.: Yale University Press, 1982), 19, 75.

44. Quoted in Van Patten, "The Partisan Battle," 399.

Madison's point here is that the intentions of the Philadelphia framers are not paramount; it is the intentions of the people of the various states, who through their representatives ratified the Constitution, that are to be given primary consideration in construing the Constitution. This only makes constitutional interpretation more complex.[45] If it is difficult to know the framers' intentions, it is even more difficult to know the intentions of all who were involved in the ratification process. Madison was apparently emphatic about this. He chose to delay publication of his notes of the Constitutional Convention until after his death, or, in his own words,

> at least, . . . till the Constitution should be well settled by practice, and till a knowledge of the controversial part of the proceedings of its framers could be turned to no improper account. . . . As a guide in expounding and applying the provisions of the Constitution, the debates and incidental decisions of the Convention can have no authoritative character.[46]

In Madison's view, then, constitutional interpretation should rely on the intentions of the state ratifiers, not those who sat in Philadelphia.[47] One scholar has expressed the opinion that Madison's view was prevalent in the late eighteenth and early nineteenth centuries; that is, in the nation's early years, the original intent relevant to constitutional discourse was not that of the Philadelphia framers, but rather that of the several parties to the constitutional compact—the states as political entities.[48]

Alexander Hamilton's view of constitutional interpretation likewise did not look principally to the framers, but neither did it look to the ratifiers. Instead, Hamilton looked to the Constitution itself. Hamilton was committed to giving to the Constitution, in the tradition of

---

45. Ibid.

46. Letter from James Madison to Thomas Ritchie (15 September 1791); reprinted in Philip B. Kurland and Ralph Lerner, eds., *The Founders' Constitution*, 5 vols. (Chicago: University of Chicago Press, 1987) 1: ch. 2, No. 28, p. 74.

47. Van Patten, "The Partisan Battle," 399.

48. H. Jefferson Powell, "The Original Understanding of Original Intent," *Harvard Law Review* 98 (March 1985): 888.

common law rules of construction, its face meaning: "Whatever may have been the intention of the framers of a Constitution, or of a law, that intention is to be sought for in the instrument itself, according to the usual and established rules of construction . . . [and] arguments drawn from extrinsic circumstances . . . must be rejected."[49]

This conclusion from the general principles of legal interpretation was confirmed, Hamilton added, by the language of the Constitution itself, in the necessary and proper clause:[50] "The whole turn of the clause, . . . indicates, it was the intent of the convention, by that clause to give a liberal latitude to the exercise of the specified powers."[51] For Hamilton, then, the Constitution speaks for itself; there is no need to go behind it to ascertain the intent of the framers. However, in what it says, the Constitution is liberal in its granting of powers to the national government.

Thomas Jefferson advocated still another method of constitutional interpretation—the rule of strict constructionism. Jefferson strongly asserted that the Constitution was grounded on the principle embodied in the Tenth Amendment: that all undelegated powers are reserved "to the states respectively, or to the people."[52] For Jefferson, the principle of states' rights was supreme among the intentions of the framers, and thus should be strictly adhered to.[53] Accordingly, Jefferson's view of constitutional interpretation was in one way similar to Hamilton's. Under both views, the intentions of the framers are apparent in the words of the Constitution. They differed, however, on the point of what the document said. Hamilton saw liberal powers granted to the new national government; Jefferson saw a very limited grant of power to the national government.

---

49. Quoted in ibid., 915.

50. U.S. Constitution, Article I, Section 8: "The Congress shall have Power . . . to make all laws which shall be necessary and proper for carrying into Execution the foregoing Powers and all other Powers vested by this Constitution in the Government of the United States, or in any Department or Officer thereof."

51. Alexander Hamilton, "Opinion on the Constitutionality of an Act to Establish a Bank" (1791), reprinted in *Papers of Alexander Hamilton*, Harold C. Syrett, ed. (New York: Columbia University Press, 1961), 102-03; quoted in Powell, "The Original Understanding," 916.

52. U.S. Constitution, Amendment X.

53. Powell, "The Original Understanding," 916-17.

In the first half of the nineteenth century, two conflicting approaches to constitutional interpretation emerged, roughly paralleling the differences expressed by Hamilton, on the one hand, and Jefferson, on the other. The nationalist school, championed by Daniel Webster and Justice Joseph Story, explicitly rejected the Jeffersonian definition of the Constitution as a compact among sovereign states. The nationalists regarded the Supreme Court as the final and authoritative interpreter of the Constitution. John C. Calhoun headed the states' rights school, insisting that final interpretive authority rested with the states. Adherents of both camps, however, expressed their views as explications of the "original intent" of the framers, leaving behind earlier reluctances, such as those expressed by Madison, against the use of "extrinsic evidence" in constitutional interpretation.[54]

Immediately following the Civil War, a virtually uniform appeal to the framers' "original intent" reigned supreme. States' rights advocates continued to appeal to the intentions of the framers in support of their views. Yet nationalists were equally vocal in their advocacy for a methodology of constitutional interpretation that stressed the intention of the framers. Senator Charles Sumner of Massachusetts, reputedly one of the most radically nationalist members of the Union Congress, stated: "Every Constitution embodies the principles of its framers. It is a transcript of their minds. If its meaning in any place is open to doubt . . . we cannot err if we turn to the framers. . . ."[55]

The Union victory in the Civil War signaled a Union repudiation of the Confederacy's emphasis on states' rights; the Reconstruction witnessed an unprecedented era of statutory and constitutional lawmaking, greatly expanding the federal government's power to invade areas traditionally reserved to the states. Since that time, the struggle over the federal/state balance of power has been largely resolved in favor of virtually plenary federal power.[56] The Reagan administration's proposals to return power to the states dramatically demonstrated the appeal of "a written constitution with a fixed meaning . . . to limit

---

54. Ibid., 945-46.
55. *Congressional Globe*, 39th Congress, 1st Session, 677 (1866); quoted in Powell, "The Original Understanding," 947.
56. Powell, "The Compleat Jeffersonian," 1321-22.

the arbitrary exercise of governmental power."[57] The return of power to the states has been recently championed on the Supreme Court by William Rehnquist, who frequently calls for a return to the framers with statements like the one he made in *Nevada* v. *Hall*:[58] "We must examine further the understanding of the Framers and the consequent doctrinal evolution of concepts of state sovereignty."[59]

The presence of federalism as a strand of American political thought that has its roots in Philadelphia has never passed out of national view. It emphasizes the "original intent" of the framers to protect the freedoms of the states and their citizens by reserving to them the power and authority to secure their freedoms. Contemporary adherents of this strand of political emphasis continue to emphasize the original intentions of the framers as essential to constitutional interpretation. Yet strong nationalists also continue to appeal to the original intentions of the framers to support their own political emphasis. William Brennan, for example, appeals to the need for the judiciary to interpret the Constitution in a way that accommodates social progress, but also accommodates original intent: "We look to the history of the timing of the framing *and* to the intervening history of the interpretation."[60]

In light of the historic and contemporary appeals from both sides for the necessity of a constitutional jurisprudence that upholds, to one degree or another, the intentions of the framers, it is altogether proper to consider the intentions of the framers. Moreover, the Supreme Court has historically considered the intentions of the founding fathers, when discoverable, to be important, if not binding, in constitutional interpretation. This is as it should be, of course. The Constitution is the national charter of the United States. It is the binding framework of law for the nation; all other laws must be measured by it; it is the starting place for a people committed to the rule of law in a civilized society. Therefore, its original meanings, if ascertainable, neces-

---

57. Edwin Meese, speech given to the Federalist Society in Washington, D.C., 30 January 1987; reprinted in *Marquette Law Review* 70 (Spring 1987): 380-88.

58. 440 U.S. 410 (1979).

59. Ibid., 433-34 (Rehnquist, J., dissenting).

60. Address by William J. Brennan, "The Constitution," 433 (emphasis added).

sarily govern its interpreters.

No one denies that there are considerable tensions between text and intent in the Constitution; but where intent can be investigated so as to illumine text, it is an altogether proper inquiry. Nor should anyone approach the intent of the framers as being so fixed as to prevent some measure of freedom to constitutional interpreters. The American Constitution would not have survived for more than two hundred years if it was not a flexible document. It has been the peculiar genius of the Constitution that, while its provisions are sufficiently detailed to provide a necessary element of stability to government, it has nonetheless proved to be broad and general enough to allow for steady growth to meet the altered requirements of an ever changing social order.[61] So while the notion of a "living constitution" is valid, the American Constitution would someday lose all of its meaning if its primary guardians, the justices of the United States Supreme Court, were not committed to its original meanings. Thus original intent is not always the final answer in constitutional interpretation, but it is a very important starting place.

This commitment to original intent is especially valid with respect to the religion clauses. An understanding of the original intent of the founding fathers with respect to the role of religion in America is a "necessary first step in reading the religion clauses of the Constitution."[62] The founding fathers were closer to the problem of religious despotism, having seen its effects in Europe and in the colonies. Their aspirations of providing guarantees for religious liberty in a constitutional government are instructive to a contemporary America that retains those aspirations. Thus it is exceedingly important to consider the intentions of the framers, who so significantly began the First Amendment with the provisions concerning religion.[63]

---

61. Kelly and Harbison, *The American Constitution*, 2.

62. Jonathan K. Van Patten, "In the End Is the Beginning: An Inquiry into the Meaning of the Religion Clauses," *Saint Louis University Law Journal* 27 (February 1983): 5.

63. Robert T. Miller and Ronald B. Flowers, *Toward Benevolent Neutrality: Church, State and the Supreme Court*, 3rd ed. (Waco, Tex.: Baylor University Press, 1987), 3.

Chapter 4

THE RELIGION CLAUSES AND THE ORIGINAL INTENT OF THE FRAMERS

Interpreting the Religion Clauses: The Quest for Original Intent

The first sixteen words of the First Amendment to the U.S. Constitution provide: "Congress shall make no law respecting an establishment of religion, or prohibiting the free exercise thereof." The first ten words are commonly referred to as the Establishment Clause; the last six are often referred to as the Free Exercise Clause; together they are frequently referred to as "the religion clauses."

The religion clauses are intimately interrelated in their purposes. It may be said that the framers' central purpose in both clauses was to protect religious liberty—to prohibit the coercion of religious practice or conscience, a goal that remains paramount today.[1] Justice Brennan's examination of the religion clauses in one case resulted in this conclusion:

> The two clauses, although distinct in their objectives and their applicability, emerged together from a common panorama of history. The inclusion of both restraints . . . shows unmistakably that the

---

1. See *Engel* v. *Vitale*, 370 U.S. 421 (1962), 429-30; *Zorach* v. *Clauson*, 343 U.S. 306 (1952), 313-14; *Everson* v. *Board of Education*, 330 U.S. 1 (1947), 8-11; Leo Pfeffer, *Church, State and Freedom*, 2nd ed. (Boston, Mass.: Beacon Press, 1967), 122; Jesse H. Choper, "The Religion Clauses of the First Amendment: Reconciling the Conflict," *University of Pittsburgh Law Review* 41 (Spring 1980): 677.

Framers of the First Amendment were not content to rest the protection of religious liberty exclusively upon either clause.[2]

The two clauses, on their face, express twin foci: the prohibition of an establishment of religion and the guarantee of the free exercise of religion. The first clause prohibits; the second clause protects. In the words of one authority, the clauses express "a tradition of freedom *of* religious exercise and a tradition of freedom *from* religious exercise."[3] The clauses issue two separate mandates. The Establishment Clause was clearly intended to eliminate the possibility of an established church in the new nation; beyond that, full agreement as to the framers' intent ceases.[4] There is less disagreement about the purpose of the Free Exercise Clause. It was intended to preserve the right of the citizen to believe, in the words of John Locke, "according to the dictates of his own Conscience,"[5] free from civil coercion.

Because the meaning of the Establishment Clause is less clear than the meaning of the Free Exercise Clause, most of the contemporary debate over the framers' intent in the wording of the religion clauses focuses on the Establishment Clause. Furthermore, the debate tends to revolve around the Establishment Clause because the key issues focus upon the degree of permissible government sponsorship, promotion, advancement, or support of religious activities, and it is accepted by all that the term "establishment" as contained in the Establishment Clause bears most directly upon this issue. This is not to say, of course, that the Free Exercise Clause is free from debate on its original meaning, as will become more than evident in the course of this volume, but only that it receives less attention than the controversy regarding the original meaning of the Establishment Clause.

Regarding the Establishment Clause, there are two basic interpretations of what the constitutional framers intended it to mean: the broad

---

2. *Abington School District v. Schempp*, 374 U.S. 203 (1963), 232 (Brennan, J., concurring).

3. Van Patten, "The Meaning of the Religion Clauses," 32 (emphasis in original).

4. Miller and Flowers, *Toward Benevolent Neutrality*, 241.

5. John Locke, "A Letter Concerning Toleration" (1685), reprinted in *Main Currents of Western Thought*, ed. Franklin Le Van Baumer, 4th ed. (New Haven, Conn.: Yale University Press, 1978), 355.

interpretation and the narrow interpretation.[6] The broad interpretation was first advanced by Justice Hugo Black for a five-to-four majority in the 1947 landmark case of *Everson* v. *Board of Education*.[7] In what is certainly the most frequently quoted portion of any Supreme Court opinion dealing with church-state issues, Justice Black declared:

> The "establishment of religion" clause of the First Amendment means at least this: Neither a state nor the Federal Government can set up a church. Neither can pass laws which aid one religion, aid all religions, or prefer one religion over another. Neither can force nor influence a person to go to or to remain away from church against his will or force him to profess a belief or disbelief in any religion. No person can be punished for entertaining or professing religious beliefs or disbeliefs, for church attendance or non-attendance. No tax in any amount, large or small, can be levied to support any religious activities or institutions, whatever they may be called, or whatever form they may adopt to teach or practice religion. Neither a state nor the Federal Government can, openly or secretly, participate in the affairs of any religious organizations or groups and vice versa. In the words of Jefferson, the clause against establishment of religion by laws was intended to erect "a wall of separation between church and State."[8]

Relying upon the intent of the framers, the Court thus declared that the original purpose of the Establishment Clause was to create an absolute separation of the spheres of civil authority and religious activity by forbidding all forms of government assistance or support

---

6. Leonard W. Levy, "The Original Meaning of the Establishment Clause of the First Amendment," in *Religion and the State: Essays in Honor of Leo Pfeffer*, ed. James E. Wood, Jr. (Waco, Tex.: Baylor University Press, 1985), 43. Regarding the broad and narrow views of interpretation, some would say that to place all views of church-state relationships into only two categories is an oversimplification. Actually, the two-category model is inferred from the *Everson* case in which Justice Hugo Black referred to the Court's adoption of the "broad meaning" and the "broad interpretation" of the Establishment Clause. See 330 U.S. 1, 15. However, Professor Carl Esbeck has provided five very insightful and useful categories to differentiate various perceptions of the proper relationship between government and religion. His categories, explained in his article, are: strict separationists, institutional separationists, pluralistic separationists, nonpreferentialists, and restorationists. See Esbeck, "Five Views of Church-State Relations in Contemporary American Thought," *Brigham Young University Law Review* 86 (Fall 1986): 371-404.

7. 330 U.S. 1 (1947).

8. Ibid., 15-16.

for religion. That is, the clause went far beyond merely intending to prohibit the governmental establishment of a single church or of preferring one religious sect over another. As Leonard Levy has stated, "The heart of this broad interpretation is that the First Amendment prohibits even government aid impartially and equitably administered to all religious groups."[9]

This "broad" interpretation is also sometimes referred to as the "separationist" or "no aid" approach. That is, there is to be strict separation between civil authority and religion; no church or religious group should receive any form of governmental aid. This view is said to grow out of the views of many of the leaders in the movement for religious liberty, notably Thomas Jefferson and James Madison. For example, in Jefferson's "Bill for Establishing Religious Freedom" (1779) (see Appendix A) and Madison's "Memorial and Remonstrance" (1785) (see Appendix B), the idea is clearly expressed, in a number of ways, that religion should be totally independent of government interference.[10] According to Leo Pfeffer, "In the minds of the fathers of our Constitution, independence of religion and government was the alpha and omega of democracy and freedom."[11]

In contrast to the broad interpretation, the narrow interpretation holds that the framers intended for the Establishment Clause to prevent governmental establishment of a single sect or denomination of religion over others.[12] According to this interpretation, J. M. O'Neill has said that the framers purposed to prohibit "a formal, legal union of a single church or religion with government, giving the one church or religion an exclusive position of power and favor over all other churches or denominations."[13] Sometimes called "accommodationists" or "non-preferentialists," proponents of this view would permit governmental aid to religious institutions as long as it was imparted without discrimination. The framers, they contend, intended only to keep the

---

9. Levy, "The Original Meaning," 44.
10. Miller and Flowers, *Toward Benevolent Neutrality*, 242.
11. Pfeffer, *Church, State, and Freedom*, 127.
12. Levy, "The Original Meaning," 44.
13. J. M. O'Neill, *Religion and Education Under the Constitution* (New York: Harper and Row, 1949), 56.

government from abridging religious liberty by discriminatory practices generally or by favoring one denomination or sect over others. Accommodationists hold that the wall of separation between church and state "was not intended . . . to create a sharp division between government and religion or to enjoin government from fostering religion in general."[14] Accommodationists conclude that the founders intended only to remove religious requirements for public office, prevent the creation of a national church or religion, protect freedom of conscience in matters of religion against invasion by the national government, and leave the states to deal with the questions of religion as they saw fit.

It should be pointed out, too, parenthetically, that a few writers use "accommodation" in a different way, referring to the viewpoint that government should not impede or in any way stand in the way of religion. This usage, as a term used to argue for the intended relationship between government and religion, finds its meaning in an emphasis upon the Free Exercise Clause rather than the Establishment Clause. "Accommodationism," as used here as well as throughout this book, however, carries the meaning that government should encourage and support religion so long as it is done in a nondiscriminatory manner.[15] The latter usage, as a term used to argue for the intended relationship between government and religion, finds its meaning centered in the Establishment Clause, rather than the Free Exercise Clause. The differences are subtle but important for anyone reading literature referring to "accommodation" of religion in government spheres.

A leading scholar who subscribes to the accommodationist viewpoint is Robert L. Cord. His book, *Separation of Church and State: Historical Fact and Current Fiction*, is a prominent work in support of this view. Cord concludes:

> There appears to be no historical evidence that the First Amendment was intended to preclude Federal government aid to religion when it was provided on a nondiscriminatory basis. Nor does there appear to be any historical evidence that the First Amendment was intended

---

14. Levy, "The Original Meaning," 44.

15. One writer who adopts the less frequently used description is Michael W. McConnell, "Accommodation of Religion," *1985 Sup. Ct. Rev.* 1.

to provide an *absolute separation or independence* of religion and the national state.[16]

The accommodationist view is the viewpoint of Chief Justice William Rehnquist. Cord asserts, moreover, in an article in the *National Review*, that the historical analysis of the framing of the First Amendment offered by Justice Rehnquist in his dissenting opinion in *Wallace v. Jaffree*[17] drew heavily on Cord's book, a claim not altogether supportable from a reading of Rehnquist's opinion, despite the fact that Rehnquist's opinion does cite Cord's book.[18] In any case, the views of Cord and Rehnquist regarding the framing of the religion clauses appear to be substantially the same.

The broad and narrow interpretations are clearly at odds with one another. A resolution of the controversy is hampered by the fact that it is not an easy task to ascertain precisely the intent of the framers. The available sources are often unclear and, for the most part, incomplete. Moreover, as Professor Laurence Tribe has made clear, such history as there is reflects several varying purposes.[19] This uncertainty regarding the framers' intent can be seen in a brief review of the proceedings that produced the religion clauses of the First Amendment.

The Framing of the Religion Clauses and the Pursuit of Religious Liberty

The Constitutional Convention

The religion clauses contained in the First Amendment grew out of the concern of the states that the Constitution of 1787 gave little

---

16. Robert L. Cord, *Separation of Church and State: Historical Fact and Current Fiction* (New York: Lambeth Press, 1982), 15 (emphasis in original).

17. 105 S. Ct. 2479 (1985).

18. Robert L. Cord, "Correcting the Record," *National Review* (11 April 1985): 42. For Rehnquist's reference to Cord's book, see 105 S. Ct. 2479, 2515 (Rehnquist, J., dissenting).

19. Laurence H. Tribe, *American Constitutional Law* (Mineola, N.Y.: Foundation Press, 1978), Section 14-3.

attention to the subject of religion. In contrast to the Declaration of Independence, the Constitution contained no references to God. Its only reference to religion was the prohibition against religious tests for federal officeholders contained in Article VI, clause 3: "No religious test shall ever be required as a qualification to any office or public trust under the United States." Only Roger Sherman of Connecticut disapproved of the provision, not because he disagreed with its purpose and effect, but because he thought including the provision in the Constitution was "unnecessary, the prevailing liberality being a sufficient security against such tests."[20]

According to James E. Wood, Jr., this provision "precluded the possibility of any church-state union or the establishment of a state church."[21] This is an important recognition. In the absence of the provision, Congress might have had the power to compel subscription to the tenets of a particular church, or to Protestantism, or to Christianity, or to any other religion, in order to hold office.[22] Instead, the provision rendered one's religion irrelevant to a capacity to serve the country in any official sense.

No further discussions on the subject of religion occurred at the Constitutional Convention. The absence of such references in the available records of the Convention is one proof that the fifty-five delegates were little concerned with the question of religion;[23] another proof is the almost total absence of any discussion of religion in The Federalist. Written to draw support for ratification of the new Constitution, only James Madison in The Federalist made a single reference to religion by mentioning "a zeal for different opinions concerning religion" as one of the "latent causes of faction" that appear in civil society.[24] The framers, it could be argued, believed that religion was

20. James Madison, Notes of Debates in the Federal Convention of 1787, ed. Adrianne Koch (Athens, Ohio: Ohio University Press, 1966), 561.

21. James E. Wood, Jr., " 'No Religious Test Shall Ever Be Required': Reflections on the Bicentennial of the U.S. Constitution," Journal of Church and State 29 (Spring 1987): 200.

22. Levy, "The Original Meaning," 45.

23. Leonard W. Levy, The Establishment Clause: Religion and the First Amendment (New York: Macmillan, 1986), 63-65; Levy, "The Original Meaning," 45-46.

24. Quoted in Anson Phelps Stokes, Church and State in the United States, 3 vols. (New York: Harper, 1950) 1:532.

none of the business of the national government; it was best left to the states.[25] According to this view, Congress was powerless, even in the absence of the First Amendment, to enact laws that aided religion.[26]

The Convention delegates soundly rejected a proposal by George Mason of Virginia to include a Bill of Rights in the Constitution. The almost uniform belief of the delegates was that a Bill of Rights would be superfluous. The new federal government possessed only limited powers delegated to it by the states; no power had been granted to legislate on any of the subjects that might be included in a Bill of Rights. Because no such power existed, none could be exercised or abused, and therefore an enumeration of provisions against that possibility was unnecessary.[27] In the words of Alexander Hamilton in *The Federalist*: "For why declare that things shall not be done which there is no power to do? Why, for instance, should it be said that the liberty of the press shall not be restrained, when no power is given by which restrictions may be imposed?"[28] It would be the states, though, fearful of a national government that would arrogate power unto itself, that would insist upon specific protections for individual freedoms, including religious liberty.

Ratification Controversy

From late 1787 until 1789, the proposed Constitution was considered by the various state-ratifying conventions. A strong anti-federalist element developed quickly; it opposed ratification, fearing that the new document's centralizing tendencies would crush the rights of states and individuals. For many of the states, the only solution to this problem was to mandate the inclusion of a bill of rights in the Constitution. Indeed, six of the thirteen states—Massachusetts, New Hampshire, North Carolina, New York, Rhode Island, and Virginia[29]—accompanied their instruments of ratification with a list of recommended amendments that

---

25. Ibid.
26. Levy, "The Original Meaning," 46.
27. Ibid.
28. *The Federalist*, No. 84.
29. Levy, "The Original Meaning," n. 14.

would secure various personal liberties, such as "rights of conscience," "liberty of the press," and "rights of trial by jury."[30] However, the records of the debates of the state ratifying conventions are of little help in ascertaining the precise meanings that such liberties were to assume. Leonard Levy has suggested that the debate that took place over a bill of rights, both public and in the ratifying conventions themselves, "was conducted on a level of abstraction so vague as to convey the impression that Americans during 1787-88 had only the most nebulous conception of the meanings of the particular rights they sought to secure."[31].

Of the six states that recommended amendments to secure personal liberties, all but Massachusetts submitted proposals regarding religious freedom. Massachusetts, which maintained multiple establishments of religion at the time,[32] was the first state to ratify with amendments, but the only personal rights mentioned were those of the criminally accused. Massachusetts assemblymen obviously did not feel that the Massachusetts religious establishments were in any way threatened by the proposed Constitution; they believed that the new federal government was to be impotent in matters of religion.[33]

New Hampshire recommended the following amendment: "Congress shall make no laws touching Religion, or to infringe the rights of Conscience."[34] However, because the records of the debates in the New Hampshire assembly are nonexistent, little can be known about how the New Hampshire delegates understood the need, purpose, and parameters of their proposal.

In Virginia, James Madison argued that no amendments to the Constitution were necessary. His efforts failed, however, and among the amendments recommended was one providing that "no particular religious sect or society ought to be favored or established, by law, in preference to others."[35]

---

30. Ibid., 46-47.

31. Ibid., 47.

32. Jonathan Elliott, *The Debates in the Several State Conventions on the Adoption of the Federal Constitution*, 5 vols. (Philadelphia: J. P. Lippincott, 1941) 2:236.

33. Ibid.

34. Charles C. Tansill, ed., *Documents Illustrative of the Formation of the Union of the American States* (Washington D.C.: Government Printing Office, 1927), 1026.

35. Ibid., 1031; Elliott, *Debates*, 3:659.

In New York, not a single word of the week-long debate is recorded. Accordingly, the Convention members left no explanation of what they understood by their proposed amendment "that no Religious Sect or Society ought to be favored or established by Law in preference of others."[36] This wording was the same as that used in the state constitution of 1777, which abolished religious establishments in New York.[37]

North Carolina, which had abolished its Anglican establishment in 1776, recommended an amendment virtually identical to those of Virginia and New York.[38] Rhode Island offered a similar proposal against establishment modeled after those of Virginia, New York, and North Carolina.[39]

It is clear from the amendments proposed by the various states that none favored the establishment of religion by Congress. But what *was* an establishment of religion that was to be beyond the federal exercise of power? Did it mean that only a national church, sect, or denomination was not to be established? Or did it mean more—the prohibition of support of any church, sect, or denomination, or even religion in general? The evidence does not permit a conclusive generalization of what was meant by an establishment of religion. It is apparent that the states wanted to reserve jurisdiction over religion to themselves—indeed, many maintained establishments of religion—and the federal government was not to meddle in religious matters. Whether or not the Congress was to be prohibited from offering any type of nondiscriminatory financial support to churches, however, or even to promote religion in general, is unclear from an examination of the debates of the state ratifying conventions. Surely the First Congress would deal with these issues with considerably more precision.

---

36. Tansill, *Documents*, 1035.
37. Levy, "The Original Meaning," 51.
38. Tansill, *Documents*, 1047. Levy presents a brief, but cogent account of the debates of the New York convention regarding the matter of religious liberty. See Levy, "The Original Meaning," 51-52.
39. Tansill, *Documents*, 1053.

The First Congress and the Emergence of the Religion Clauses

James Madison had been among those who argued that a bill of rights was unnecessary. He insisted that the national government had no power to infringe upon individual rights. He soon came to appreciate the honest fears of the delegates to the state conventions, however, who insisted upon a clear prohibition of federal infringement upon the rights of conscience as well as other individual liberties. Most of the states were willing to ratify the Constitution largely because of Madison's assurances that, at the First Congress, he would seek to secure the kinds of amendments they wanted.[40]

After the Constitution was ratified, Madison, feeling "bound in honor" to secure amendments,[41] was true to his word and offered a number of proposed amendments to the First Congress to allay the apprehension of many of the states. On 8 June 1789, at the opening of the First Congress, Representative Madison proposed, among others, the following amendment: "The civil rights of none shall be abridged on account of religious belief, nor shall any national religion be established, nor shall the full and equal rights of conscience in any manner or in any respect be infringed."[42]

Proponents of the narrow interpretation of the Establishment Clause claim that the word "national" is proof that Madison intended nothing more than a prohibition against the preference of one religion over another. Robert Cord, for example, argues that Madison's proposal supports his thesis that

> the religion clauses ultimately adopted by Congress were meant to deny to Congress the constitutional authority to pass legislation

---

40. James E. Wood, Jr., E. Bruce Thompson, and Robert T. Miller, *Church and State in Scripture, History, and Constitutional Law* (Waco, Tex.: Baylor University Press, 1958), 101-02.

41. Annals of the Congress of the United States, *The Debates and Proceedings in the Congress of the United States*, 42 vols., compiled from authentic materials by Joseph Gales, Sr. (Washington, D.C.: Gales and Seaton, 1834) 1:441; reprinted in Kurland and Lerner, *The Founder's Constitution*, 5: Bill of Rights, No. 11, 21-32.

42. *Annals*, 1:451, as appearing in Kurland and Lerner, *The Founder's Constitution*, 5: Bill of Rights, No. 11, 25.

> providing for the formal and legal union of any single church, religion, or sect with the Federal Government. . . . Consequently the separation of Church and the national State envisioned by the adopters of the First Amendment would leave the matter of religious establishments or disestablishment to the wisdom of the several States.[43]

On initial consideration, Cord's thesis seems persuasive. Yet there are a number of facts that suggest that Madison might have opposed more than just the establishment of a national church.

Madison had led a fight in 1785 in the Virginia legislature against a bill calling for a general tax assessment for the support of, not one, but all Christian religions. In his renowned "Memorial and Remonstrance," Madison repeatedly referred to the assessment bill as an "establishment of religion."[44] After his retirement from the presidency, Madison in 1817 expressed his disapproval of tax-supported chaplains for Congress and the armed services as well as presidential proclamations of days of thanksgiving. Significantly, he described these as "establishments" and "the establishment of national religion."[45] All of this makes it difficult to know conclusively what Madison meant when he submitted his proposed amendment prohibiting the "establishment" of a "national religion." He may have been signifying not that the federal government had no business preferring one church or religion over others but that national action on behalf of any or all churches or religions was outside the purview of permissible government action.

Madison's proposed amendment was referred to a specially formed select Committee, of which Madison was a member. The Committee changed the wording of the amendment proposal several times, but eventually settled on the following language: "No religion shall be established by law, nor shall the equal rights of conscience be infringed."[46]

---

43. Robert L. Cord, *Separation of Church and State* (1982), 5.

44. Robert A. Rutland, ed., *The Papers of James Madison*, 9 vols. (Charlottesville, Va.: University of Virginia Press, 1976) 8:298-306.

45. Elizabeth Fleet, ed., "Madison's Detached Memoranda," *William and Mary Quarterly* 3 (1946): 554-59.

46. *Annals*, 1:729; quoted in Michael J. Malbin, *Religion and Politics: The Intentions of the Authors of the First Amendment* (Washington, D.C.: American Enterprise Institute for Public Policy Research, 1978), 5.

Debate on the Select Committee's proposed amendment opened on 15 August 1789. Peter Sylvester, a fifty-year-old lawyer from New York, opened the debate and focused on the establishment question. He feared that the clause "might be thought to have a tendency to abolish religion altogether."[47] Michael Malbin has suggested that Sylvester had two premises in mind as he spoke:

> (1) He probably was concerned that the phrase "no religion should be established by law" could be read as a prohibition of all direct or indirect governmental assistance to religion, including land grants to church schools, such as those contained in the Northwest Ordinance, or religious tax exemptions. (2) Sylvester apparently thought some form of governmental assistance to religion was essential to religious survival. Unless these premises are assumed, it is difficult to see how Sylvester could have seen the establishment clause as a threat to religion.[48]

Malbin, then, finds in these two premises evidence that the House was concerned that the proposed amendment would prohibit nondiscriminatory governmental aid to various forms of religion. This gives support to his own view of the historical meaning of the Establishment Clause: Congress desired to encourage religion, which led them to accept nondiscriminatory aid to religion.[49] Yet there would seem to be at least one more plausible explanation for Sylvester's stated concern. Sylvester may have been concerned that the proposed amendment might be construed by the American people as a congressional outlawing of religion altogether. If that was the essence of Sylvester's thinking, which is altogether possible from a literal reading of the Committee's proposal, he was not concerned with the issue of governmental aid to religion, as Malbin suggests, but with the much larger issue of the very survival of religion. In that case, he would merely be asking for a rephrasing of the amendment; his comment would say nothing about his views on establishment.

The debate continued. The only account of the debate, in the

---

47. *Annals*, 1:729, quoted in Malbin, *Religion and Politics*, 7.
48. Malbin, *Religion and Politics*, 7.
49. Ibid., 7, 40.

Annals of Congress, is given in paraphrased form. Levy's description is lugubrious:

> It [the debate] proves nothing conclusively. It was apathetic and unclear: ambiguity, brevity, and imprecision in thought and expression characterized the comments of the few members who spoke. That the House understood the debate, cared deeply about its outcome, or shared a common understanding of the finished amendment is doubtful.[50]

The House, acting as a Committee of the whole, concluded the debate, and upon a motion by Samuel Livermore of New Hampshire passed a revised amendment proposal: "Congress shall make no laws touching religion, or infringing the rights of conscience." Five days later, on 20 August, Fisher Ames of Massachusetts moved that the amendment read: "Congress shall make no law establishing religion, or to prevent the free exercise thereof, or to infringe the rights of conscience." Without debate, this proposal was adopted by the necessary two-thirds of the House. The amendment as submitted to the Senate, however, reflected a stylistic change that gave it the following reading: "Congress shall make no law establishing religion, or prohibiting the free exercise thereof, nor shall the rights of conscience be infringed." No record was left of the proceedings that brought about this stylistic change.[51]

The Senate began deliberations on the House amendment on 3 September and continued through 9 September. The Ames amendment must have provoked controversy in the Senate, since several alternative versions were suggested in its place. In considering the House's draft, a Senate motion was first made to strike out "religion, or prohibiting the free exercise thereof," and to insert, "one religious sect or society in preference to others."[52] The motion was first rejected, and then passed.[53] Thus, the first new Senate version read: "Congress shall make

---

50. Levy, "The Original Meaning," 58.

51. *Annals,* 1:796; all quotes are from Levy, "The Original Meaning," 59.

52. Linda Grant DePauw, ed., *Documentary History of the First Federal Congress of the United States of America,* 3 vols. (Baltimore: Johns Hopkins University Press, 1971) 1: 151.

53. Ibid.

no law establishing one religious sect or society in preference to others, nor shall the rights of conscience be infringed."[54]

After further debate, the Senate rejected two alternative wordings. First, they rejected language providing: "Congress shall not make any law, infringing the rights of conscience, or establishing any Religious Sect or Society."[55] Second, they rejected language providing: "Congress shall make no law establishing any particular denomination of religion in preference to another, or prohibiting free exercise thereof, nor shall the rights of conscience be infringed."[56]

Considerable disagreement exists among church-state scholars as to the meaning that should be given these Senate drafts. For example, Levy,[57] as well as Douglas Laycock, argue that all three of these drafts favored the "no preference" viewpoint, but all were rejected because the Senate clearly wanted a wording favoring the broad interpretation of the Establishment Clause. Laycock comments: "At the very least, these three drafts show that if the First Congress intended to forbid only preferential establishments, its failure to do so explicitly was not for want of acceptable wording. The Senate had before it three very clear and felicitous ways of making the point."[58] Gerard Bradley, however, holding to the narrow interpretation, seems to suggest that the rejected versions all were aimed at prohibiting a national church, indicating, despite the fact that all three versions were rejected, the dominant idea among the Senators—no national church.[59]

Later the same day, 3 September, the Senate adopted a draft that treated religion more generically: "Congress shall make no law establishing religion, or prohibiting the free exercise thereof."[60] Six

---

54. Ibid.

55. Ibid.

56. Ibid.

57. Levy, "The Original Meaning," 60.

58. Douglas Laycock, " 'Nonpreferential' Aid to Religion: A False Claim About Original Intent," *William and Mary Law Review* 27 (Special Issue 1985-86), 880. Also, see Douglas Laycock, "Original Intent and the Constitution Today," in *The First Freedom: Religion and the Bill of Rights*, ed. James E. Wood, Jr. (Waco, Tex.: Dawson Institute of Church-State Studies, 1990): 87-112.

59. Gerard V. Bradley, *Church-State Relationships in America* (Westport, Conn.: Greenwood Press, 1987), 93-94.

60. DePauw, *Documentary History*, 1:151.

days later, the Senate again changed its mind and adopted, as its final form of the amendment: "Congress shall make no law establishing articles of faith or a mode of worship, or prohibiting the free exercise of religion."[61] Like the three defeated motions, however, this has the unmistakable meaning of prohibiting acts that prefer one church or sect over others—clearly a narrow intent.

The Senate version of the amendment was then sent to the House, which rejected it. Levy has suggested that this action indicates that the House was not satisfied with merely a ban on the preference of one church or sect over another—clearly, according to Levy, a broad intent.[62]

A House-Senate joint conference committee was then created to resolve the disagreement over the religion amendment. A compromise amendment was eventually agreed upon on 25 September and passed by both branches: "Congress shall make no law respecting an establishment of religion, or prohibiting the free exercise thereof."[63] The joint committee left no records of their deliberations, but the congressional action was completed. The religion clauses had been approved as the first sixteen words of the First Amendment.

The First Amendment, with eleven other amendments, were submitted to the thirteen state legislatives for ratification. Much to the disappointment of students of American constitutional law, records of the states' debates are nonexistent. By June 1790, the necessary nine states had approved of ten amendments—the Constitution's Bill of Rights.[64]

The Search for Meaning

The foregoing account is but a brief sketch of the historic developmental phases that eventually produced the religion clauses of the First Amendment. Excellent, more detailed accounts are available.[65] The account

---

61. Ibid., 1:166.
62. Levy, 59-60.
63. *Annals*, 1:913; DePauw, *Documentary History*, 1:181.
64. Levy, 61-65.
65. For example, Leonard Levy's book, *The Establishment Clause*, gives a thorough account of the broad interpretation. Also presenting this view are Leo Pfeffer, *Church*,

provided here is not intended as an argument for either a broad or narrow interpretation of the religion clauses (Rehnquist's interpretation, as well as this author's evaluation of that interpretation, are covered in later chapters); the point here is that in all of the developmental process, the framers left no record of any attempts to define terms so as to enable succeeding generations to determine with precision the intended meaning of the religion clauses. What is an "establishment"? What is a law "respecting" an establishment of religion? What is meant by the word "religion," or of the "free exercise thereof"? Moreover, extrapolation on the meaning of such terms is frustrated by the paucity of records of the debates in Congress and the state ratifying conventions.

One writer has said that the "men who wrote the Constitution wrote under great duress and heightened pressure; they developed the document in a politically charged environment and were subject to compromise and negotiation. . . ."[66] Philip Kurland, in considering the enterprise of discovering the framers' original intent in fashioning the religion clauses, has written: "At best, the past is never fully recapturable, and the parts that are recapturable may not be an accurate reflection of what actually happened. When the quarry is neither recorded words nor events, but rather the state of mind that gave rise to the words or events, and when the state of mind is not of one person but of many persons, the pursuit of the past is almost hopeless."[67] Regarding the debates of the First Congress, Levy adds: "Not even Madison himself, dutifully carrying out his pledge to secure amendments, seems to have troubled to do more than was necessary

---

State and Freedom; Stokes, Church and State in the United States; and Thomas Curry, The First Freedoms: Church and State in America to the Passage of the First Amendment (Oxford: Oxford University Press, 1986). The best-known works presenting the narrow interpretation are Chester James Antieu, Arthur L. Downey and Edward C. Roberts, Freedom from Federal Establishment Formation and Early History of the First Amendment Religion Clauses (Milwaukee: Bruce Publishing Company, 1964); Walter Berns, The First Amendment and the Future of American Democracy (New York: Basic Books, 1976); Malbin, Religion and Politics; Cord, Separation of Church and State; and Bradley, Church-State Relationships in America.

66. Ball, "The Convergence of Constitutional Law," 886.

67. Philip B. Kurland, "The Origins of the Religion Clauses of the Constitution," William and Mary Law Review 27 (Special Issue, 1985-86), 860.

to get something adopted in order to satisfy popular clamor and deflate anti-federalist charges."[68]

Despite the absence of perspicuous meanings in the religion clauses, seemingly every writer who embarks upon the arduous task of ascertaining the original intent of the framers in their crafting of the religion clauses concludes that his or her interpretation is the right one. The subject, apparently because of its implications in the formation of public policy—especially in education—seems to transform into partisans all who approach it. The issue is, however, certainly more debatable than partisans on either side would have anyone believe. Close scrutiny of all of the available records yields many helps, but not irrefutable conclusions.[69]

The Supreme Court has historically considered the original intent of the framers of the religion clauses a salient matter. A historical overview, in the next chapter, of how the Court has interpreted the religion clauses will provide the final foundation block for the consideration of William Rehnquist's own interpretations.

68. Levy, "The Original Meaning," 58.
69. Ibid., 44.

Chapter 5

THE SUPREME COURT IN AMERICAN HISTORY AND THE UNCERTAIN CRITERIA OF ORIGINAL INTENT

The Supreme Court has often resorted to an examination of the original intent of the framers in its efforts to interpret the meanings of the religion clauses.[1] This commitment by the Court to the use of history as a guide indicates a commendable degree of objectivity and detachment. In the area of religion, a lack of commitment to history would open the Court to accusations of subjective bias either for or against religion. Accordingly, the Court's effort to examine the origins of the religion clauses reflects its understanding of the need to consider authorities independent of itself.[2]

Like all who make the effort to determine the framers' intentions with respect to the religion clauses, however, the Court has struggled. In its efforts to reconcile two clauses that are sometimes complemen-

---

1. See, for example, *Reynolds* v. *U.S.*, 98 U.S. 145 (1878), 162-64; *Everson* v. *Board of Education*, 330 U.S. 1 (1947), 8-13; ibid., 33-43 (Rutledge, J., dissenting); *McCollum* v. *Board of Education*, 333 U.S. 203 (1948), 213-15 (Frankfurter, J., concurring); ibid., 244-48 (Reed, J., dissenting); *Engel* v. *Vitale*, 370 U.S. 421 (1962), 425-36.

2. Van Patten, "The Meaning of the Religion Clauses," 6. See also Charles A. Miller, *The Supreme Court and the Uses of History* (Cambridge, Mass.: Belknap Press of Harvard University, 1969), 26-28.

tary, sometimes conflicting,[3] the Court's "wall of separation,"[4] which is "high and impregnable,"[5] often becomes "serpentine"[6] and "porous."[7] The Court's difficult task of developing a coherent, consistent approach to the role of religion in a democracy[8]—one that is true to the original intent of the framers—can readily be seen in a review of a selection of noteworthy cases. All of the cases treated in this chapter antedate William Rehnquist's 1971 appointment to the Court; thus they form an armamentarium of Supreme Court perspectives on the framers' purposes that Rehnquist, in time, would forcefully critique.

The Mormon Cases

The religion clauses had only a small impact on church-state relations during the entire history of the United States before 1940, since prior to that time those clauses only applied to the federal government.[9] Unlike the majority of the personal liberties guaranteed in the Bill of Rights, the religion clauses were clearly directed at limiting the power of the national government.[10] Thus some states maintained official religious establishments well into the nineteenth century.[11] All states eventually adopted nonestablishment provisions; such provisions

3. A. E. Dick Howard, "The Wall of Separation: The Supreme Court as Uncertain Stonemason," in *Religion and State: Essays in Honor of Leo Pfeffer,* ed. James E. Wood, Jr., 101.

4. *Everson* v. *Board of Education,* 330 U.S. 1 (1947), 16.

5. Ibid., 18.

6. "Church-State Separation: A Serpentine Wall?" *Christianity Today,* 6 July 1962, 29-31.

7. Howard, "The Wall of Separation," 110.

8. Van Patten, "The Meaning of the Religion Clauses," 6.

9. See, for example, *Permoli* v. *Municipality No. 1 of the City of New Orleans,* 44 U.S. (3 How.) 589 (1845), 609: "The Constitution makes no provision for protecting the citizens of the respective states in their religious liberties; this is left to the state constitutions and laws: nor is there any inhibition imposed by the Constitution of the United States in this respect on the states."

10. *Barron* v. *Baltimore,* 32 U.S. (7 Pet.) 243 (1833), in which the Supreme Court, by holding that the Fifth Amendment was inapplicable to the states, implied that all of the Bill of Rights were likewise inapplicable to the states.

11. The last official establishment, the Congregational establishment in Massachusetts, was abolished in 1833.

were generally drafted and interpreted to preclude only direct aid to religion.[12] The passage of the Fourteenth Amendment in 1868 had no immediate impact upon state practices; religious matters continued to be handled under state laws.[13]

The emergence of the Mormons in the Western territories, however, raised the question of governmental regulation of religious activities. George Reynolds, private secretary to Brigham Young, was convicted in 1875 in the Utah Territory for violating a federal statute prohibiting polygamy. Reynolds invoked the Free Exercise Clause as a defense, contending that polygamy was his religious duty. In 1878, in *Reynolds* v. *United States*,[14] the Supreme Court affirmed the conviction and rejected the religious freedom defense. The Court determined the scope of protection for religious freedom by relying upon "the history of the times in the midst of which the provision was adopted."[15] The Court examined Madison's "Memorial and Remonstrance," Jefferson's Virginia "Statute for Religious Freedom," and Jefferson's 1802 letter to the Danbury Baptist Association containing the "wall of separation" metaphor. All of the texts were cited for the proposition that there was an unqualified freedom for beliefs, but not actions. "Congress was deprived of all legislative power over mere opinion, but was left free to reach actions that were in violation of social duties or subversive of good order."[16] In the Court's view, polygamy violated institutional marriage, a most important feature of social life and order. The Court supported the government's power to regulate polygamy.

Polygamy did not die easily in the territories. Twelve years later, in *Davis* v. *Beason*,[17] the regulation of polygamy in the Idaho Territory was the issue. The Court again looked to history for an understanding of the purposes—and limits—of the First Amendment:

---

12. Pfeffer, *Church, State and Freedom*, 141-42.

13. Van Patten, "The Meaning of the Religion Clauses," 8; Mark DeWolfe Howe, *The Garden and the Wilderness: Religion and Government in American Constitutional History* (Chicago: University of Chicago Press, 1965), 72-73.

14. 98 U.S. 145 (1878).

15. Ibid., 162.

16. Ibid., 164.

17. 133 U.S. 333 (1890).

The oppressive measures adopted, and the cruelties inflicted by the governments of Europe for many ages, to compel parties to conform in their religious beliefs and modes of worship to the views of the most numerous sect, and the folly of attempting in that way to control the mental operations of persons and enforce an outward conformity to a prescribed standard, led to the adoption of the Amendment in question. It was never intended or supposed that the Amendment could be invoked as a protection against legislation for the punishment of acts inimical to the peace, good order and morals of society.[18]

In extending the belief-action dichotomy, the Court said, in effect, that believing in polygamy was acceptable, but practicing it was not.[19]

Incorporation of the Religion Clauses Through the Due Process Clause of the Fourteenth Amendment

In *Gitlow* v. *New York*,[20] the Supreme Court formally recognized that the Due Process Clause might make certain provisions of the Bill of Rights applicable to the states. In that case, the Court incorporated First Amendment free speech and press guarantees. The Court deemed such guarantees "fundamental rights and 'liberties' protected by the due process clause of the Fourteenth Amendment from impairment by the States."[21] After *Gitlow*, incorporation continued on a case-by-case basis.[22]

---

18. Ibid., 342.

19. The "belief-action" test, which has its roots in the Jeffersonian concept of free exercise, is an extremely narrow definition of the constitutional guarantee of religious free exercise. It has never been overruled by the Court, but it has never again been advanced as the sole standard for testing the limits of "free exercise," and since 1970 has seldom been cited as controlling. An excellent article discussing these points is by Rodney K. Smith, "Getting Off on the Wrong Foot and Back on Again: A Reexamination of the History of the Framing of the Religion Clauses of the First Amendment and a Critique of the *Reynolds* and *Everson* Decisions," *Wake Forest Law Review* 20 (Fall 1984): 569-642.

20. 268 U.S. 652 (1925).

21. Ibid., 666.

22. Regarding the incorporation process, see Charles Fairman, *The Fourteenth Amendment and the Bill of Rights* (New York: De Capo Press, 1970); also Charles

In *Cantwell* v. *Connecticut*,[23] members of the Jehovah's Witnesses were arrested under a Connecticut statute requiring a license for the solicitation of funds. The statute, which gave broad censorship powers to state officials, was held to be an invalid restriction on the defendants' free exercise of religion. The Court's basis for the holding was that the Free Exercise Clause was applicable to the states: "The fundamental concept of liberty embodied in that [Fourteenth] Amendment embraces the liberties guaranteed by the First Amendment."[24]

The *Cantwell* case was monumental in its effects. Because the Free Exercise Clause was now binding on the states, it would usher in a new era of Supreme Court jurisdiction over religion in America. The Court, however, offered no historical analysis of either the First Amendment or the Fourteenth Amendment, or their relationship to each other.[25]

In *Everson* v. *Board of Education*,[26] the Supreme Court extended the incorporation doctrine to the Establishment Clause. A New Jersey statute had provided that state tax money could be used to reimburse parents for the cost of transporting children by bus to parochial schools. A taxpayer challenged the statute as a violation of the Establishment Clause, claiming that such payments were an impermissible advancement of religion. The Court, with Justice Black writing for the majority, expressly held that the Establishment Clause applied to the states, but ruled that the reimbursements were not a violation of the clause. Justice Black's majority opinion, as well as Justice Rutledge's dissenting opinion, included extensive examinations of the historical events leading up to and culminating in the adoption of the religion clauses. Their

---

Fairman, "Does the Fourteenth Amendment Incorporate the Bill of Rights? The Original Understanding," *Stanford Law Review* 2 (1949): 5-139; and Stanley Morrison, "Does the Fourteenth Amendment Incorporate the Bill of Rights? The Judicial Interpretation," *Stanford Law Review* 2 (1949): 140-73.

23. 310 U.S. 2967 (1940).

24. Ibid., 303.

25. Mark DeWolfe Howe notes that there was no discussion of the Fourteenth Amendment's possible impact on religion during the congressional debates leading to its passage, and that accordingly, religious matters continued for decades thereafter to be handled exclusively by the states. See Howe, *The Garden and the Wilderness*, 72-90.

26. 330 U.S. 1 (1947).

similar historical analyses, however, led to opposite conclusions.

Black began his analysis by noting that many of the early colonists came to America to escape religious persecutions. However, many of the colonial establishments were not formed on the principle of religious freedom. Religious minorities, especially Catholics, Quakers, and Baptists, underwent considerable persecution for their religious beliefs.[27] Black described those persecutions as the inaugurator of a movement for religious freedom: "These practices became so commonplace as to shock the freedom-loving colonials into a feeling of abhorrence. The imposition of taxes to pay ministers' salaries and to build and maintain churches and church property aroused their indignations. It was these feelings which found expression in the First Amendment."[28]

For Black, the struggle and the victories ultimately won for religious freedom in Virginia were especially influential on the framers as they fashioned the religion clauses. Jefferson's "Statute for Religious Freedom," passed in 1786, not only ended the Anglican establishment in Virginia but also prohibited state support of religion and made religion a private, not civil, concern.[29] Together with Madison's "Memorial and Remonstrance," written in 1785 in opposition to a renewal of a tax to support the Anglican establishment, Jefferson's "Statute" furnished the Court with evidence of the principles underlying the religion clauses: "This court has previously recognized that the provisions of the First Amendment, in the drafting and adoption of which Madison and Jefferson played such leading roles, had the same objective and were intended to provide the same protection against governmental intrusion on religious liberty as the Virginia Statute."[30]

The Court thus reasoned that the framers considered "an establishment of religion" to mean more than the mere establishment of a national church—it meant, generally, any governmental intrusion on religious liberty. In keeping with this broad interpretation, Black then listed a number of hypothetical violations of the Establishment Clause, and included among them the requirement that "no tax in

---

27. Ibid., 10.
28. Ibid., 11.
29. Wood, Thompson, and Miller, *Church and State*, 93-94.
30. 330 U.S. 1 (1947), 13.

any amount, large or small, can be levied to support any religious activities or institutions. . . ."[31] He concluded, however, that reimbursements to parents from state tax revenues were not tantamount to tax levies for religious activities; therefore, there was no Establishment Clause violation. According to Black, to deprive the parents of reimbursement for transportation costs bordered closely on an infringement of free exercise.[32]

Justice Rutledge's dissent also tracked the significant contributions of Jefferson, and especially Madison, as leaders of the Virginia march toward full religious liberty. He cited Madison's "Remonstrance" as "at once the most concise and the most accurate statement of the views of the First Amendment's author [Madison] concerning what is 'an establishment of religion' "[33] Rutledge believed the "Remonstrance" to be a forceful argument against any form of governmental aid to religion. In turn, the primary concern of Congress, according to Rutledge, was not preserving power to use public funds in support of religion, but rather making sure that the language adopted was not so broad as to restrict the free exercise of religion.[34] Accordingly, Rutledge's understanding of the original intent of the framers was virtually identical to that of Black. Rutledge, however, contrary to Black, concluded that the New Jersey reimbursement program was the type of support of religion that the framers intended to forbid.

The Released-Time Cases

The next major church-state case after *Everson* was *McCollum v. Board of Education*.[35] In that case the Court declared that a plan to offer released-time religious education on school grounds during the school day violated the Establishment Clause. As in *Everson*, Justice Black wrote the majority opinion; he relied heavily upon the strict separa-

---

31. Ibid., 16.
32. Ibid.
33. Ibid., 37 (Rutledge, J., dissenting).
34. Ibid., 42.
35. 333 U.S. 203 (1948).

tionist rhetoric laid out in *Everson*.

Justice Felix Frankfurter's concurring opinion in *McCollum* is interesting in two respects. First, he attempted to show that the non-sectarian, public school format functions best in an environment of separation, where there is an intentional effort to respect the divergent religious beliefs of the students. After tracing the historical development of the public school concept, he concluded: "The public school system is at once the symbol of our democracy and the most pervasive means for promoting our common destiny. In no activity of the State is it more vital to keep out divisive forces than in its schools, to avoid confusing, not to say fusing, what the Constitution sought to keep strictly apart. . . ."[36]

Second, Justice Frankfurter presented a new, as well as unique argument for the propriety of the incorporation doctrine:

> Long before the Fourteenth Amendment subjected the States to new limitations, the prohibition of furtherance by the State of religious instruction became the guiding principle, in law and feeling, of the American people. . . .
>
> Separation in the field of education, then, was not imposed upon unwilling States by force of superior law. In this respect the Fourteenth Amendment merely reflected a principle then dominant in our national life. To the extent that the Constitution thus made it binding upon the States, the basis of the restriction is the whole experience of our people.[37]

Here, Frankfurter was advancing the idea that the religion clauses applied to the states, in spirit, long before the adoption of the Fourteenth Amendment. The Fourteenth Amendment merely codified, at least with respect to the field of education, what the people already recognized: government at any level should not advance religion. This is, to be sure, different from the usual incorporation argument, which advances the idea that in the adoption of the Fourteenth Amendment Congress enacted safeguards for liberty that only came to be recognized

---

36. Ibid., 231 (Frankfurter, J., concurring).
37. Ibid., 215.

approximately seventy-five years later.[38]

Four years later, the Court gave evidence that it was struggling to enunciate clear guidelines as to how the Establishment Clause should be interpreted. In *Zorach* v. *Clauson*,[39] the Court approved a New York City program of released-time because the instruction took place away from school grounds and there was no coercion to get the children to participate. Furthermore, there was no expenditure of state funds in the administration of the program. The Court's opinion, written by Justice William O. Douglas, sounded like a radical departure from its separationist approach in *Everson* and *McCollum*:

> We are a religious people whose institutions presuppose a Supreme Being. We guarantee the freedom to worship as one chooses. We make room for as wide a variety of beliefs and creeds as the spiritual needs of man deem necessary. . . . When the state encourages religious instruction or cooperates with religious authorities by adjusting the schedule of public events to sectarian needs, it follows the best of our traditions. For it then respects the religious nature of our people and accommodates the public service to their spiritual needs. To hold that it may not would be to find in the Constitution a requirement that the government show a callous indifference to religious groups. That would be preferring those who believe in no religion over those who do believe.[40]

Justice Black, one of the three dissenters, disagreed that there was no coercion. He saw New York City using "its compulsory education laws to help religious sects get attendants presumably too unenthusiastic to go unless moved to do so by the pressure of this state machinery."[41] He concluded: "Government should not be allowed, under cover of the soft euphemism of 'co-operation,' to steal into the sacred area of religious choice."[42]

---

38. Van Patten, "The Meaning of the Religion Clauses," 19; also see Pfeffer, *Church, State and Freedom*, 142-44; and Alexander Bickel, "The Original Understanding and the Segregation Decision," *Harvard Law Review* 69 (1955): 64-65.

39. 343 U.S. 306 (1952).

40. Ibid., 313-14.

41. Ibid., 318 (Black, J., dissenting).

42. Ibid., 320.

The *Zorach* majority opinion made no appeal to history and the intent of the framers. However, the Court did appear to be shifting toward a flexible, "accommodationist" approach to Establishment Clause interpretation.

The Sunday Closing Cases

On the same day in 1961, 29 May, the Supreme Court handed down four decisions upholding the constitutionality of state Sunday closing laws. Two of the cases were decided on Establishment Clause grounds; two were decided on Free Exercise Clause grounds.[43] In deciding all of the cases, the Court used the "argument from history."[44] Although the laws originally had a religious purpose (Sabbath observance), they had been secularized in that they had come to be regarded only as laws recognizing a common day of rest for a working citizenry.

The *McGowan* case contained an extensive discussion of the historical background of the Sunday closing laws and their compatibility with the First Amendment.[45] Chief Justice Earl Warren focused on the Virginia experience, noting that Sunday work proscriptions were not believed to be inconsistent with the Virginia Declaration of Rights enacted in 1776.[46] In addition, James Madison, who led the movement for Anglican disestablishment in Virginia, introduced a bill in the Virginia legislature for the punishment of "Sabbath Breakers." The law passed in 1785 and remained in effect during the time that Madison fought for the First Amendment in Congress.[47] Warren considered

---

43. The establishment claims were *McGowan* v. *Maryland*, 366 U.S. 420 (1961), and *Two Guys From Harrison-Allentown, Inc.* v. *McGinley*, 366 U.S. 582 (1961). The free exercise claims were *Braunfeld* v. *Brown*, 366 U.S. 599 (1961), and *Gallagher* v. *Crown Kosher Super Market of Mass.*, 366 U.S. 617 (1961).

44. For an excellent discussion of the "argument from history" rationale in relation to the Sunday closing cases, see Miller and Flowers, *Toward Benevolent Neutrality*, 289-92.

45. Justice Frankfurter also wrote a lengthy (84 pages) concurring opinion in which he delved deeply into the history of Sunday labor laws and their compatibility with the First Amendment.

46. 366 U.S. 420 (1961), 438.

47. Ibid.

the congressional proceedings that framed the religion clauses and concluded that "the First Amendment, in its final form, did not simply bar a congressional enactment *establishing a church*; it forbade all laws *respecting an establishment of religion*."[48] Because Madison's career showed great sensitivity to the slightest encroachments upon religious liberty, he could not have, according to Warren, deemed the Virginia Sunday labor prohibitions as a violation of the First Amendment.[49] In his consideration of the purpose of the First Amendment, Warren opined that its goals were broader than those stated by nineteenth-century Chief Justice Joseph Story. Story's view was that the "real object of the amendment was . . . to prevent any national ecclesiastical establishment, which should give to an hierarchy the exclusive patronage of the national government."[50]

The Demise of Official Prayer in the Public Schools

In 1962, the Supreme Court issued a decision that was one of the most controversial in its history. In *Engel* v. *Vitale*,[51] the Court struck down a twenty-two word, nondenominational prayer written by the New York State Board of Regents for official use in the public schools of New York.[52] Local school boards were not required to use the prayer; it was merely a recommended prayer that each school board could implement for daily classroom recital if it chose to do so. Justice Black, in writing for the Court, rejected the argument that, since the prayer was nonsectarian and since the pupils could remain silent or be excused from the room if they requested, there was no constitutional violation. Black stated:

---

48. Ibid., 441-42 (emphasis in original).

49. Ibid., 438-41.

50. Ibid., 441, quoting Joseph Story, *Commentaries on the Constitution of the United States*, 3:728.

51. 370 U.S. 421 (1962).

52. The prayer read: "Almighty God, we acknowledge our dependence upon Thee, and we beg thy blessing upon us, our parents, our teachers, and our country"; ibid., 422.

The Establishment Clause, unlike the Free Exercise Clause, does not depend upon any showing of direct governmental compulsion and is violated by the enactment of laws which establish an official religion whether those laws operate directly to coerce non-observing individuals or not. . . .

The Establishment Clause . . . stands as an expression of principle on the part of the Founders of our Constitution that religion is too personal, too sacred, too holy, to permit its "unhallowed perversion" by a civil magistrate.[53]

Justice Black purposed to rely upon history and the founding fathers for the result in *Engel*. He began by assuring that "it is a matter of history that this very practice of establishing governmentally composed prayers for religious services was one of the reasons which caused many of our colonists to leave England and seek religious freedom in America."[54] The *Book of Common Prayer*, intended as a unifying document for the Church of England, asserted Black, became the focal point of intense religious controversy. The imposition of the orthodoxy of the Church of England, said Black, led many to flee the Mother Country and, unfortunately, impose their own orthodoxy in America. Gradually, continued Black, there developed in America an intense opposition to religious domination. By the time of the ratification of the Constitution and the Bill of Rights, there was an awareness throughout the colonies of the dangers of a union of church and state.[55] The First Amendment was adopted "to stand as a guarantee that neither the power nor the prestige of the Federal Government would be used to control, support or influence the kinds of prayer the American people can say—that the people's religions must not be subjected to the pressures of government for change each time a new political administration is elected to office."[56]

Black went on to describe many of the founding fathers as men with "faith in the power of prayer."[57] Thus his argument seemed

---

53. Ibid., 430, 432.
54. Ibid., 425.
55. Ibid., 429.
56. Ibid., 429-30.
57. Ibid., 434-35.

to be that the framers believed in prayer, but not prayer promulgated by civil authority. The argument operates only by analogy, however, as there is no evidence whatsoever on what the framers intended with regard to public school prayer. As Justice O'Connor later noted in a concurring opinion in *Wallace* v. *Jaffree*:[58] "[Because] there then existed few government-run schools, it is unlikely that the persons who drafted the First Amendment . . . anticipated the problems of interaction of church and state in the public schools."[59]

Justice Potter Stewart was the only dissenter in the six-to-one decision in *Engel* (Justice Frankfurter was ill and Justice White was not yet on the bench when the case was argued). He attacked Black's argument by reminding his Court brethren that Washington, Adams, Jefferson, and Madison, all founding fathers, included prayers in their first official presidential acts.[60] These important examples, to be sure, are good evidence that at least some of the founding fathers did not believe some forms of public prayer to be unconstitutional. Caution should be exercised, however, in making such examples dispositive on the issue of prayer in an altogether different setting, the public schools.

The Founding Fathers and the Formulation of Establishment Clause Guidelines

Despite considerable public vilification of the Supreme Court following its *Engel* decision,[61] the Court agreed in 1963 to hear two more cases dealing with religion in the public schools. *Abington Township School District* v. *Schempp*[62] involved a Pennsylvania statute providing that at least ten Bible verses should be read daily in each public school

---

58. 105 S. Ct. 2479 (1985).

59. Ibid., 2503 (O'Connor, J., concurring).

60. 370 U.S. 421 (1962), 445 n. 3 (Stewart, J. dissenting).

61. For a sampling of the various reactions to the *Engel* case, see "Uproar Over School Prayer—And the Aftermath," *U.S. News and World Report,* 9 July 1962, 42-44, and James E. Wood, Jr., "Religion Sponsored by the State," *Journal of Church and State* 4 (November 1962): 141-49.

62. 374 U.S. 203 (1963).

classroom in the state. Reading was to be without comment and students could request to be excused. The other case, *Murray v. Curlett*,[63] challenged a Maryland statute that provided for the daily reading of a chapter from the Bible and/or recitation of the Lord's Prayer in the state's public schools. The two cases were decided together under the *Schempp* title. The Court disallowed the practices in both cases as violations of the Establishment Clause.

The Court's opinion, by Justice Tom Clark, began by affirming the religious character of the American people and suggested that it had always been that way: "The Founding Fathers believed devotedly that there was a God and that the unalienable rights of man were rooted in Him."[64] Clark continued: "This is not to say, however, that religion has been so identified with our history and government that religious freedom is not likewise as strongly imbedded in our public and private life."[65] The "belief in liberty of religious opinion" espoused by Roger Williams, James Madison, and Thomas Jefferson "came to be incorporated . . . in the Federal Constitution."[66] Clark failed to give any particulars of the views of Williams, Madison, and Jefferson regarding religious liberty, but argued, in effect, that their views called for a "neutral" position toward all religious opinions and sects. The Court held that the implicit endorsement of religion in the state—mandated Bible reading and reciting of the Lord's Prayer violated this neutrality.[67]

Anyone reading Justice Clark's opinion will discover that he actually relied more on *Everson, McCollum,* and *Engel* than he did on the original intent of the framers. This may be the natural effect of the building of an inventory of precedents, but in a concurring opinion, Justice Brennan signaled the need for a more acutely intentional shift away from the history of the First Amendment. Brennan warned: "A too literal quest for the advice of the Founding Fathers upon the issues of these cases seems to me futile and misdirected. . . ."[68] As justification

63. Ibid.
64. Ibid., 213.
65. Ibid., 214.
66. Ibid.
67. Ibid., 223-24.
68. Ibid., 237 (Brennan, J., concurring).

for his advice, Brennan cited the ambiguities in the historical record, changes in American practices—such as educational formats—since the First Amendment was adopted, and the greater religious diversity in contemporary society than among the forefathers. In applying these factors to the facts of the cases before him, Brennan stated:

> Whatever Jefferson or Madison would have thought of Bible reading or the recital of the Lord's Prayer in what few public schools existed in their day, our use of the history of their time must limit itself to broad purposes, not specific practices. By such a standard . . . the devotional exercises carried on in the Baltimore and Abington schools offend the First Amendment because they sufficiently threaten in our day those substantive evils the fear of which called forth the Establishment Clause of the First Amendment. It is "*a constitution we are expounding*," and our interpretation of the First Amendment must necessarily be responsive to the much more highly charged nature of religious questions in contemporary society.[69]

At least one scholar, Jonathan Van Patten, has argued that Brennan's suggestions in *Schempp* provided a basis for a marked shift in the Court's willingness to engage in historical analysis. Van Patten suggested that the early reliances upon Madison and Jefferson have faded from the Court's opinions since *Schempp*, opting instead for the key principle of "neutrality" in Establishment Clause cases.[70]

There is also in the *Schempp* case the clear indication that the Court was beginning to move toward specific guidelines for deciding Establishment Clause cases. The Court set forth two specific tests that any legislation must be measured against to determine its constitutionality. Justice Clark wrote:

---

69. Ibid., 241 (emphasis in original).

70. Van Patten, "The Meaning of the Religion Clauses," 26. Van Patten supports his argument, in part, by an examination of *Sherbert* v. *Verner*, 374 U.S. 398 (1963), a free exercise case decided on the same day as *Schempp*. In *Sherbert*, the Court held that a state may not deny unemployment compensation to an employee who refused to work on her Sabbath. The majority opinion, written by Justice Brennan, contains no historical analysis. Van Patten suggested that this omission was intentional, and indicated that the Court was beginning to put some distance between itself and the founding fathers.

The test may be stated as follows: what are the purpose and the primary effect of the enactment. If either is the advancement or inhibition of religion then the enactment exceeds the scope of legislative power as circumscribed by the Constitution. That is to say that to withstand the strictures of the Establishment Clause there must be a secular legislative purpose and a primary effect that neither advances nor inhibits religion.[71]

Having enunciated the "secular purpose" and "primary effect" tests in *Schempp*, the Court in 1970 added a third test in *Walz* v. *Tax Commission*,[72] the "excessive entanglement" test. In upholding tax exemptions for properties used for religious worship, Chief Justice Warren Burger reasoned for the Court: "Granting tax exemptions to churches necessarily operates to afford an indirect benefit and also gives rise to some, but yet a lesser, involvement than taxing them. In analyzing either alternative the questions are whether the involvement is excessive, and whether it is a continuing one calling for official and continuing surveillance leading to an impermissible degree of entanglement."[73]

The *Walz* test of "excessive entanglement" was formally placed with the *Schempp* tests of "secular purpose" and "primary effect" in *Lemon* v. *Kurtzman*,[74] and the three are thus commonly referred to collectively as the "*Lemon* three-prong test." The three component parts of the test stand independent of each other. Thus the failure of legislation to pass any of the three tests will render it violative of the Establishment Clause.

It is interesting to note that Chief Justice Burger's opinion in *Walz* made no examination of the original intent of the framers. Rather, he placed reliance upon the Court's previous gloss on the meanings of the religion clauses. Justice Brennan, however, who had given indications in *Schempp* that searching for the framers' original intent was sometimes risky, made an extensive reading of history in his concurring opinion. According to Brennan, the Court's decision must be one that "accords with history and faithfully reflects the under-

---

71. 374 U.S. 203, 222.
72. 397 U.S. 664 (1970).
73. Ibid., 674-75.
74. 411 U.S. 192 (1973).

standing of the Founding Fathers."[75] Brennan examined the widespread practice of granting tax exemptions that had prevailed from the time of the birth of the nation and found that the practice was not only prevalent but uncontroversial. Yet he discovered no record of the views of the two most prolific founding fathers, Thomas Jefferson and James Madison. He concluded: "The absence of such a record is significant. It is unlikely that two men so concerned with the separation of church and state would have remained silent had they thought that exemptions established religion."[76]

Walz and the "Neutral Course" Between the Religion Clauses

Walz v. Tax Commission[77] was an important decision also from the standpoint of its discussion of the tensions between the Establishment Clause and the Free Exercise Clause. Walz went further than any previous Supreme Court case in forging certain principles that might serve as a set of guidelines for the resolution of conflicts between the two religion clauses. The conflicts were the result of prior holdings in a number of significant cases.

In Sherbert v. Verner,[78] the Court had held that a state could not deny unemployment compensation to an employee, a Seventh-day Adventist, who refused to work on Saturday, her Sabbath day. To withhold such benefits would place an undue burden on her religious beliefs in violation of the Free Exercise Clause. The state was unable to demonstrate a "compelling interest" sufficient to override the employee's free exercise rights.

Given the broad readings of the Establishment Clause in Everson, McCollum, Engel, and Schempp, and the broad reading of the Free Exercise Clause in Sherbert, "the Court appeared to be on a collision course."[79]

---

75. 397 U.S. 664 (1970), 680 (Brennan, J., concurring).
76. Ibid., 684-85.
77. 397 U.S. 664 (1970).
78. 374 U.S. 398 (1963).
79. Van Patten, "The Meaning of the Religion Clauses," 26.

The Court's prohibitions against advancing religion, on the one hand, and the requirement that religious beliefs must be respected, on the other hand, forcefully produced conflict between the religion clauses.

In *Walz*, the petitioner argued that real estate tax exemptions for religious organizations were tantamount to a direct subsidy and therefore in violation of the Establishment Clause. The Court held this was not an establishment and indicated that churches or other religious organizations may have free exercise claims. Chief Justice Burger stated: "Nothing in this national attitude toward religious tolerance and two centuries of uninterrupted freedom from taxation has given the remotest sign of leading to an established church or religion and on the contrary it has operated affirmatively to help guarantee the free exercise of all forms of religious belief."[80] In focusing on this inherent conflict between the two religion clauses, Burger made the rather forthright admission that the "Court has struggled to find a neutral course between the two Religion Clauses, both of which are cast in absolute terms, and either of which, if expanded to a logical extreme, would tend to clash with the other."[81]

Tax exemptions, without even being taken to their logical extremes, are technically religious establishments. Yet the requirements to respect the free exercise claims of churches are considerable, if not overwhelming. Burger summed up the Court's solution to this paradox:

> The course of constitutional neutrality in this area cannot be an absolutely straight line; rigidity could well defeat the basic purpose of these provisions, which is to insure that no religion be sponsored or favored, none commanded, and none inhibited. The general principle deducible from the First Amendment and all that has been said by this Court is this: that we will not tolerate either governmentally established religion or governmental interference with religion. Short of those expressly proscribed governmental acts there is room for play in the joints productive of a benevolent neutrality which will permit religious exercise to exist without sponsorship and without interference.[82]

---

80. 397 U.S. 664 (1970), 678.
81. Ibid., 668-69.
82. Ibid., 669.

Burger's "benevolent neutrality" doctrine is an extension of the "neutrality" position of *Schempp*, only more flexible. The goal of achieving the demands of both of the religion clauses, according to Burger, is not an easy one. Yet the uneasy, uncertain path of "benevolent neutrality" is, Burger suggests, the best course. For Burger, it is a course consistent with the objective of the framers in drawing the First Amendment religion clauses—namely, "to state an objective, not to write a statute."[83]

83. Ibid., 668.

Chapter 6

REHNQUIST'S PERSPECTIVE ON THE RELIGION CLAUSES AND THE ORIGINAL INTENT OF THE FRAMERS

Rehnquist: A Voice for Accommodation

William Rehnquist has frequently criticized the Supreme Court for its reading of the original intent of the founding fathers in relation to the religion clauses. For Rehnquist, this misreading by the Court is the product of a "callous indifference to religious groups"[1] and a tendency to prefer "those who believe in no religion over those who do believe."[2] Rehnquist has accused the Court of going beyond an expressed commitment to neutrality toward religion by throwing "its weight on the side of those who believe our society as a whole should be a purely secular one."[3] These are the kind of criticisms that could be made only by one fully convinced of the need for the Supreme Court to chart a new course.

For Rehnquist, most of the Supreme Court's misdoing has resulted from its faulty interpretation of the Establishment Clause. Rehnquist has clearly adopted an accommodationist, nonpreferentialist interpre-

---

1. *Meek* v. *Pittenger*, 421 U.S. 349 (1975), 396 (Rehnquist, J., dissenting); quoting from Justice William O. Douglas's majority opinion in *Zorach* v. *Clauson*, 343 U.S. 306 (1952), 314.
2. Ibid.
3. 421 U.S. 349 (1975), 395 (Rehnquist, J., dissenting).

tation of the Establishment Clause. In *Wallace* v. *Jaffree*,[4] Rehnquist wrote a lengthy dissent calling for a total revamping of the Court's interpretation of the Establishment Clause. He was unequivocal in stating the framers' purpose: "The Framers intended the Establishment Clause to prohibit the designation of any church as a 'national' one. The Clause was also designed to stop the Federal Government from asserting a preference for one religious denomination or sect over others."[5] For Rehnquist, the Court's flawed reading of history has led to "unprincipled" decisions since the 1947 *Everson* case: "The true meaning of the Establishment Clause can only be seen in its history. As drafters of our Bill of Rights, the Framers inscribed the principles that control today. Any deviation from their intentions frustrates the permanence of that charter and will only lead to the type of unprincipled decisionmaking that has plagued our Establishment Clause cases since *Everson*."[6]

Rehnquist is convinced that there is far greater room for the accommodation of religion in governmental spheres than is currently permitted by the Supreme Court. Accordingly, for Rehnquist, the notion that the Constitution requires the government to be neutral toward religion is a fiction, and government should be free to dispense nondiscriminatory aid to various religious groups. The "wall of separation" between church and state, says Rehnquist, is a "useless" metaphor that should be abandoned.[7]

In all of this, Rehnquist's underlying commitment is to the constitutional framers. For Rehnquist, only a strict adherence to the framers' intentions will reinstate the kind of interaction between religion and government that they contemplated. By examining in this chapter Rehnquist's views on the original intentions of the framers, the clear contrast between Rehnquist's views and those of many of his Court colleagues is clearly seen. Rehnquist's views, explained in this chapter under a number of judicial themes that he prominently addresses in his written Court opinions, indicate not only a Supreme Court in

---

4. 105 S. Ct. 2479 (1985).
5. Ibid., 2520.
6. Ibid.
7. Ibid., 2516-17.

some disarray about the intent of the framers but also considerable disagreement between Rehnquist and some of his fellow justices concerning the course the Court should take in resolving future church-state issues.

Strict Constructionism, Judicial Deference, and States' Rights Advocacy

The judicial doctrines previously discussed in Chapter 2—strict constructionism, judicial deference, and states' rights advocacy—are as fundamentally important in guiding William Rehnquist in the area of church-state controversies as in any other area of judicial proceedings.

Rehnquist's commitment to states' rights can be seen, for example, in the case of *Ohio Civil Rights Commission v. Dayton Christian Schools*.[8] There, an elementary school teacher in one of three Dayton Christian Schools became pregnant and informed the school that she would like to keep teaching both during her pregnancy and in the following year. She was informed that her teaching as a new parent would be in conflict with the school's philosophy that the mother should be in the home during the child's preschool years. She asked her attorney to contact the school about the matter. Shortly after receiving a letter from her attorney, the school suspended the teacher for violating her contract, which required that she follow the "biblical chain of command" for internal resolution of disputes.

The teacher filed a sex-discrimination complaint with the Ohio Civil Rights Commission, which in turn notified the school that they would begin an administrative investigation. Dayton Christian Schools then filed a suit in a federal district court seeking an injunction to bar the administrative hearings. The suit contended that the Ohio statutes permitting the administrative investigation into the school's employment practices violated both the Free Exercise Clause and the Establishment Clause.

The district court refused to issue the injunction, holding that

---

8. 106 S. Ct. 1945 (1986).

the state has a "compelling and overriding interest in eliminating sex discrimination in the employment setting."[9] However, the Sixth Circuit Court reversed the decision and ruled in favor of the school on free exercise and establishment grounds.

The Supreme Court unanimously reversed the decision of the circuit court and remanded the case for further proceedings, but the Court split five-to-four as to the appropriateness of the district court's originally assuming any jurisdiction over the case. In writing for the Court, Rehnquist cited "the proper respect for the fundamental role of States in our federal system"[10] and "federalism"[11] as prohibiting a federal court from enjoining a pending proceeding in state courts or state administrative bodies except "in the very unusual situation that an injunction is necessary to prevent great and irreparable injury."[12] Rehnquist noted that the elimination of sex discrimination is an important state interest and that the Civil Rights Commission's investigation violated no constitutional rights of the school. "Even religious schools," said Rehnquist, "cannot claim to be wholly free from state regulation,"[13] and constitutional claims could be raised in a *state* court upon completion of the administrative proceedings (emphasis added).

While Rehnquist's opinion in the *Dayton* case invoked principles of federalism and deference to state courts, his dissenting opinion in an earlier case, *Bob Jones University* v. *United States*,[14] invoked principles of judicial deference to other branches of government. Bob Jones University is located in Greenville, South Carolina. The university accepted no black students prior to 1971, believing that interracial dating and marriage were forbidden by the Bible. In 1971, however, the university began accepting black students who were married. Later, unmarried black students were admitted, but rigid university rules prohibited interracial dating or marriage, upon penalty of expulsion.

---

9. Ibid., 1946.
10. Ibid., 1950.
11. Ibid.
12. Ibid.
13. Ibid., 1951.
14. 461 U.S. 574 (1983).

In 1970, the Internal Revenue Service began a new policy of disallowing tax-exempt status (under IRC Sec. 501 [c] [3]) to private schools whose admission policies discriminated on the basis of race. On 19 January 1976, the IRS officially revoked the tax-exempt status of Bob Jones University, effective 1 December 1970, the date the university had first been notified of the new policy. The university subsequently instituted action against the government, alleging that the IRS policy of denying the university its tax-exempt status was a violation of the Free Exercise Clause of the First Amendment. At issue for the university was not only the potential loss of the right of donors to deduct contributions made to the university for income, gift, and estate tax purposes, but also the sum of $489,675.59, plus interest, which the IRS contended they were owed by the university for federal unemployment taxes since 1 December 1970.

In considering the case, the Court determined that "an institution seeking tax-exempt status must serve a public purpose and not be contrary to established public policy."[15] The Court deemed racial discrimination clearly contrary to public policy and therefore held that the revocation of the university's tax-exempt status did not violate the Free Exercise Clause despite the sincerely held religious beliefs of the university.

Once again, the Court's holding was approved by an eight-to-one majority. Justice Rehnquist was the lone dissenter. Rehnquist did not disagree that there should be a strong national policy against racial discrimination. His disagreement was with the manner in which the national policy was established—through the authority of an administrative agency, the IRS. Rehnquist thought that such a major national policy should be established only by the nation's highest legislative body, the United States Congress. The majority had considered this point and determined that Congress had been fully aware of the controversy surrounding the policy for more than a decade, and by failing to alter the IRS's policy—which it certainly had the power to do—it had, in effect, acquiesced in and ratified the IRS action. Believing that the contours of public policy should be set by

---

15. 461 U.S. 574 (1983), 586.

Congress and not by judges, Rehnquist concluded that "this Court should not legislate for Congress."[16]

Justice Rehnquist's concern that the Court might be invading the province of Congress is a distinctive characteristic of conservative constitutional jurisprudence. It is a doctrine frequently adhered to by Rehnquist—judicial deference to the legislative branch of government. This line of thought holds that judicial supremacy is an idea totally foreign to the Constitution. It frequently lays stress upon comments from The Federalist, such as Alexander Hamilton's statement that the judiciary is "the least dangerous branch"[17] and James Madison's statement that "in republican government, the legislative authority necessarily predominates."[18] It emphasizes the lawmaking authority of the representative legislative branch and the law-interpreting authority of the judicial branch, and discourages judicial tendencies to "legislate."[19] As a philosophy, it often stresses the means to a result as being more important than the result itself. It is a philosophy that is, according to Rehnquist, faithful to the purposes and intent of the framers.

William Rehnquist has advocated a greater accommodation of religious practice in the public school forum. His first written opinion calling for a rethinking of the Court's previous prohibitions on religious activities in the public schools was his dissenting opinion in Stone v. Graham.[20] The case strongly demonstrates Rehnquist's commitment to states' rights, deference, and strict constructionism.

The Stone case dealt with a Kentucky statute that required the posting of a copy of the Ten Commandments, purchased with private contributions, on the wall of each public classroom in the state. The

---

16. Ibid., 622.

17. The Federalist, No. 78.

18. The Federalist, No. 51.

19. The notion of the inferiority of the judicial branch to the legislative is frequently traced to Charles Montesquieu, especially his work The Spirit of the Laws (1748). However, the principle was considered extensively by earlier scholars, two of the most notable being Niccolo Machiavelli and John Locke. See Anthony J. Pansini, Niccolo Machiavelli and the United States of America (Greenvale, N.Y.: Greenvale Press, 1969). An excellent book grounded in this tradition is H. Wayne House, ed., Restoring the Constitution, 1787-1987: Essays in Celebration of the Bicentennial (Dallas, Tex.: Probe Books, 1987).

20. 449 U.S. 39 (1980).

petitioner claimed that the Kentucky statute violated the Establishment and the Free Exercise clauses of the First Amendment. The Supreme Court held the Kentucky practice to be in violation of the Court's three-part test stated in *Lemon* v. *Kurtzman*.[21] Under the *Lemon* three-part test, a statute is permissible under the Establishment Clause only if: (1) the statute has a secular legislative purpose; (2) the statute's primary or principal effect is one that neither advances nor inhibits religion; and (3) the statute does not foster an excessive government entanglement with religion.[22]

The Kentucky legislature had attempted to comply with the secular purpose test by requiring the following notation in small print on each display of the Ten Commandments: "The secular application of the Ten Commandments is clearly seen in its adoption as a fundamental legal code of Western Civilization and the Common Law of the United States."[23] However, the Court found that the primary purpose of posting the Ten Commandments was "plainly religious in nature,"[24] and that the legislative recitation of a supposed secular purpose could not blind the Court to its true purpose.

The Court noted that in *Abington School District* v. *Schempp*[25] it had indicated that the "study of the Bible or of religion, when presented objectively as part of a secular program of education, may not be effected consistently with the First Amendment."[26] However, the Court stated that in the Kentucky situation, the Ten Commandments were not integrated into the school curriculum in such a way that the Bible could be said to be an appropriate study of history, civilization, ethics, comparative religion, or some other discipline that might meet the *Schempp* requirements. The Court observed that if the Ten Commandments posted on a wall were to have any effect at all, it would likely be to induce students to read and meditate upon, perhaps to venerate and obey, the Ten Commandments. While perfectly acceptable as

---

21. 403 U.S. 602 (1971).
22. Ibid., 612-13.
23. 449 U.S. 39 (1980), 41.
24. Ibid.
25. 374 U.S. 203 (1963).
26. Ibid., 225.

a form of private devotion, the Court denied that such practices were permissible under the Establishment Clause.

Justices Blackmun, Stewart, Rehnquist, and Chief Justice Burger all dissented from the majority opinion. Justice Rehnquist's dissenting opinion, however, was the most detailed, and as Donald Boles has remarked, "from the standpoint of courtwatchers, far more interesting as a possible harbinger of things to come."[27]

Rehnquist was impressed by the finding of the Kentucky legislature and the Kentucky courts that the statute calling for the posting of the Ten Commandments had a secular legislative purpose. In a somewhat perplexing comment, however, he suggested that the Supreme Court's "summary rejection of a secular purpose articulated by the legislature and confirmed by the state court is without precedent in Establishment Clause jurisprudence. This court regularly looks to legislative articulations of a statute's purpose in Establishment Clause cases and accords such pronouncements the deference they are due."[28]

Rehnquist's approach is troublesome to many, as it would seemingly grant to state legislatures and courts the final word on constitutional findings instead of reserving that privilege to the United States Supreme Court. While he did not say so, Rehnquist's thinking probably reflected his desire that the Court permit the states to exercise more autonomy in running their own affairs, a philosophy he believes is consistent with the original intent of the founding fathers. It is, simply, a federalism that gives an expansive emphasis to the spirit of the Tenth Amendment.[29]

---

27. Donald E. Boles, "Religion and the Public Schools in Judicial Review," *Journal of Church and State* 26 (Winter 1984): 60; republished in James E. Wood, Jr., ed., *Religion, the State, and Education* (Waco, Tex.: Baylor University Press, 1984): 49-65.

28. 449 U.S. 39 (1980), 43-44. The case cited by Rehnquist as authority for this proposition is *Committee for Public Education and Religious Liberty* v. *Nyquist*, 413 U.S. 756 (1973).

29. The Tenth Amendment provides: "The powers not delegated to the United States by the Constitution, nor prohibited by it to the States, are reserved to the States respectively, or to the people." Justice Rehnquist gave an active, expansive reading to the Tenth Amendment in the landmark case of *National League of Cities* v. *Usery*, 426 U.S. 833 (1976), in which he interpreted the Amendment as a bar to congressional regulation of the "states as states." See *Usery*, 845.

The Incorporation Doctrine

As previously mentioned, in *Gitlow* v. *New York*,[30] the Supreme Court held that the First Amendment freedoms of speech and press were among the fundamental rights and liberties protected by the Due Process Clause of the Fourteenth Amendment from impairment by the states. The holding began a process of "selective incorporation" in which many of the Bill of Rights have been made applicable to the states through the Fourteenth Amendment. As already indicated, the Free Exercise Clause was incorporated in 1940,[31] and the Establishment Clause was similarly made applicable to the states in 1947.[32]

Because the "selective incorporation" doctrine expands the power of the federal government, it is not a development in American constitutional law favored by William Rehnquist.[33] He first enunciated his displeasure with the incorporation of the First Amendment religion clauses in the case of *Thomas* v. *Review Board of Indiana Employment Security Division*.[34]

In *Thomas*, the Supreme Court considered the question of the denial of unemployment compensation to a worker whose religious convictions prevented him from performing the kind of work assigned to him by his employer. A Jehovah's Witness, the worker quit his job with a machinery company after he was transferred from the department where he had been employed in working with steel products for industrial use to one that produced turrets for military tanks. He maintained that his religious beliefs forbade working in the production of armaments, but he was refused unemployment benefits under a

---

30. 268 U.S. 652 (1925).

31. *Cantwell* v. *Connecticut*, 310 U.S. 296 (1940).

32. *Everson* v. *Board of Education*, 330 U.S. 1 (1947). In *Everson*, as in *Cantwell*, the Court was unanimous on the incorporation issue.

33. See, for example, *Buckley* v. *Valeo*, 424 U.S. 1 (1976) (Rehnquist, J., concurring in part and dissenting in part); *First National Bank of Boston* v. *Bellotti*, 435 U.S. 765 (1978) (Rehnquist, J., dissenting); *Weber* v. *Aetna Casualty & Surety Co.*, 406 U.S. 164 (1972) (Rehnquist, J., dissenting); *Carter* v. *Kentucky*, 450 U.S. 288 (1981) (Rehnquist, J., dissenting); *Snead* v. *Stringer*, 102 S. Ct. 535 (1981) (Rehnquist, J., dissenting from denial of cert.); and *Nevada* v. *Hall*, 440 U.S. 410 (1979) (Rehnquist, J., dissenting).

34. 450 U.S. 707 (1981).

state law that denied compensation to any person voluntarily leaving a job without good cause.

The Indiana Supreme Court disagreed that the Indiana law was a burden on the worker's right to free exercise of religion. It also held that for the state to provide benefits under such circumstances would constitute an establishment of religion. The United States Supreme Court denied both rulings. Speaking for an eight-to-one majority, Chief Justice Burger ruled that "where the state conditions receipt of an important benefit upon conduct proscribed by a religious faith, or where it denies such a benefit because of conduct mandated by religious belief, thereby putting substantial pressure on an adherent to modify his behavior and to violate his beliefs, a burden on religion exists."[35] The state, Burger said, had not proved that the denial of benefits was the least restrictive means of achieving some compelling state interest. As to the establishment charge, he explained that a payment of benefits by the state would amount only to an appropriate "neutrality" toward religion.

Justice Rehnquist dissented principally because the majority was, in his view, only exacerbating the "tension" between the religion clauses, not acting to correct the tension. He cited as an ongoing cause of the tension, "the decision by this Court that the First Amendment was 'incorporated' into the Fourteenth Amendment and thereby made applicable against the States."[36] He added:

> As originally enacted, the First Amendment applied only to the Federal Government, not the government of the States. . . . The Framers could hardly anticipate *Barron* being superseded by the "selective incorporation" doctrine adopted by the Court, a decision which greatly expanded the number of statutes which would be subject to challenge under the First Amendment. Because those who drafted and adopted the First Amendment could not have foreseen . . . the incorporation of the First Amendment into the Fourteenth Amendment, we simply do not know how they would view the scope of the two clauses.[37]

---

35. Ibid., 717-18.
36. Ibid., 721.
37. Ibid., 721-22. The "*Barron*" case referred to by Justice Rehnquist is *Barron*

By 1985, however, it seemed that Rehnquist had resigned himself to living with the incorporation doctrine. In *Wallace v. Jaffree*,[38] the Court struck down an Alabama statute requiring a daily moment of silence for "meditation or voluntary prayer" in the Alabama public schools because the statute had as its primary purpose the advancement of religion. Justice Rehnquist wrote a lengthy dissent that called for a massive restructuring of the Court's interpretation of the Establishment Clause. Yet he embraced the incorporation doctrine, even if reluctantly, when he declared: "*Given* the 'incorporation' of the Establishment Clause as against the States via the Fourteenth Amendment in *Everson*, States are prohibited as well [as the federal government] from establishing a religion or discriminating between sects."[39]

Rehnquist's apparent decision to endure the reality of "incorporation" is likely more reasoned than principled. Nevertheless, the decision is significant and represents a positive development in his approach to church-state issues. To expect the Supreme Court to turn back the clock by scrapping the entire incorporation doctrine is so unrealistic as not to warrant consideration. The incorporation doctrine is so firmly fixed in American constitutional law that overthrowing it is no longer conceivable.[40]

If Rehnquist is to succeed in influencing the Court to narrow its interpretations of the religion clauses, he is likely to be more successful by arguing for an application to the states of the same kinds of restrictions on religion that were contemplated by the framers with respect to the national government. He may continue to encounter contrary opinions of the intentions of the framers, but at least he will be able to argue from a foundation on which changes in interpretation can be grounded. For example, if the framers intended in the Establishment Clause only to forbid the creation of a "national" church, Rehnquist could argue that the Establishment Clause forbids

---

v. *Baltimore*, 32 U.S. (7 Peters) 243 (1833), wherein Chief Justice John Marshall specifically held that the Bill of Rights did not apply to the states because there was no evidence that the constitutional framers intended that they apply.

38. 105 S. Ct. 2479 (1985).

39. Ibid., 2520 (emphasis added).

40. Levy, *The Establishment Clause*, 167.

the states from creating "state" churches; he should not argue that the Establishment Clause cannot reach the states because the framers intended the clause to apply only to the new national government.

In similar fashion, if he wants to accommodate a state in passing legislation that may, by some argument, deny free exercise rights, he could argue for a flexibility by the Court that permits states (without always the requirement of uniformity among all states) to handle their own affairs;[41] he should not argue that the Free Exercise Clause is inapplicable to the states. In sum, if Rehnquist has indeed abandoned his castigation of the incorporation doctrine, he has not suffered a setback, but has embraced an attitude that will enhance his efforts to forge changes in the Court's fundamental approaches to church-state relationships.

The "Wall of Separation" Metaphor

In *Everson* v. *Board of Education*,[42] Justice Hugo Black summed up his interpretation of the Establishment Clause with a quotation from

---

41. Rehnquist has, indirectly, made this very argument with respect to the Free Exercise Clause. In *Thomas*, he argued that the proper approach to the Free Exercise Clause was the approach stated in Justice Harlan's dissent in *Sherbert* v. *Verner*, 374 U.S. 398 (1963). In *Sherbert*, the Court held that South Carolina had violated the Free Exercise Clause by denying unemployment compensation to a Seventh-Day Adventist who was unable to find suitable work that did not require her to work on her Saturday Sabbath. In his dissent, Harlan argued for a policy that would permit South Carolina to single out for financial assistance one who is unavailable for work stemming from the exercise of religious convictions, but only if it "chose to do so." Harlan felt that the Court was "compelling" South Carolina to carve out special treatment to certain individuals on account of religious beliefs, which was, he felt, far too rigid an approach to the Free Exercise Clause. It would now seem, moreover, that the majoritarianism espoused by Rehnquist—that is, the belief that the states should be free to handle their own affairs through the legislative process—has become the majority view on the Court in the adjudication of free exercise claims. The landmark case of *Employment Division of Oregon* v. *Smith*, 110 S. Ct. 1595 (1990), for all practical purposes, overruled the *Sherbert* doctrine that required a "compelling state interest" to override one's free exercise rights. The *Smith* case, which is discussed in more detail in Chapter 7, replaces this standard by holding that government may offer religiously based exemptions from generally applicable laws, but that it is not required to do so. The *Smith* Court held, then, in effect, that accommodation of religious minorities should be left to the political process. Rehnquist did not write the Court's opinion, but he voted, not surprisingly, with the Court's six-to-three majority.

42. 330 U.S. 1 (1947).

a letter written by Thomas Jefferson to the Danbury Baptist Association in 1802. Black's summation concluded: "In the words of Jefferson, the clause against establishment was intended to erect a 'wall of separation' between church and State."[43] Because the "wall of separation" metaphor does not have its origin in the text of the Constitution, no small amount of learned discussion has centered around the question of whether the metaphor should even be used as a description of church-state relations. Leo Pfeffer, for example, finds the phrase useful in the dialogue over the meaning of the religion clauses even though it does not appear in the Constitution. He illustrates his view with an analogy: "The right to a fair trial is generally accepted to be a constitutional principle; yet the term 'fair trial' is not found in the Constitution."[44]

Few would quarrel with Pfeffer on this point. Many, however, including William Rehnquist, would have considerable apprehension in using the term in the way that Justice Black used it in the *Everson* case. For Black, the metaphor was a pregnant phrase that captured the founding fathers' goal of strict separation between religion and government. For Rehnquist, Black's use of the metaphor is a serious distortion of the true purpose of the founding fathers. The "wall" is, according to Rehnquist, a "faulty" premise upon which *Everson* and a host of succeeding cases have been wrongly decided.[45]

In his dissent in *Wallace v. Jaffree*,[46] Rehnquist was unrestrained in offering an explanation for his disaffection for the "wall of separation" metaphor. Rehnquist began his assault by examining Jefferson's letter to the Danbury Baptists. The full paragraph of his letter containing the "wall" metaphor (only a portion of which was quoted by Rehnquist) is reproduced here:

---

43. Ibid., 16.

44. Leo Pfeffer, *Church, State, and Freedom*, 133.

45. *School District of Grand Rapids v. Ball*, 105 S. Ct. 3216 (1985), 3231 (Rehnquist, J., dissenting).

46. 105 S. Ct. 2479 (1985). In *Jaffree*, the Supreme Court struck down an Alabama statute requiring a moment of silence "for prayer and/or meditation" in the Alabama public schools.

Believing with you that religion is a matter which lies solely between man and his God, that he owes account to none other for his faith or his worship, that the legislative powers of government reach actions only, and not opinions, I contemplate with sovereign reverence that act of the whole American people which declared that their legislature should "make no law respecting an establishment of religion, or prohibiting the free exercise thereof," *thus building a wall of separation between church and State.* Adhering to this supreme expression of the will of the nation on behalf of the rights of conscience, I shall see with sincere satisfaction the progress of those sentiments which tend to restore to man all his natural rights, convinced he has natural rights in opposition to his social duties.[47]

Rehnquist then expressed his regrets that the Establishment Clause had been "expressly freighted with Jefferson's misleading metaphor for nearly forty years."[48] He correctly alluded to the fact that Thomas Jefferson had been in France at the time the Bill of Rights was passed by Congress, and that he wrote the letter as a note of courtesy many years after the amendments were passed by Congress. Rehnquist's point was that Jefferson was more of a "detached observer" than an "ideal source" as to the meaning of the religion clauses.[49]

Rehnquist then proceeded to explain his own understanding of the religion clauses, relying heavily upon James Madison and his leading role in the debates of the First Congress over the language of the religion clauses. Rehnquist discovered a purpose in the religion clauses "far different" from the "highly simplified 'wall of separation between church and state.' "[50] The purpose of the Establishment Clause, according to Rehnquist, had a well-accepted meaning:

It forbade establishment of a national religion, and forbade preference among religious sects or denominations. . . . The Establishment

---

47. Thomas Jefferson to Danbury Baptist Association (1 January 1802), reprinted in Kurland and Lerner, *The Founder's Constitution,* 5: Amendment I (Religion), No. 58, p. 96 (emphasis added). The portion quoted by Rehnquist is at 105 S. Ct. 2479 (1985), 2509.
48. 105 S. Ct. 2479 (1985), 2509 (Rehnquist, J., dissenting).
49. Ibid.
50. Ibid.

Clause did not require government neutrality between religion nor did it prohibit the federal government from providing non-discriminatory aid to religion. There is simply no historical foundation for the proposition that the Framers intended to build the "wall of separation" that was constitutionalized in *Everson*.[51]

Rehnquist noted that the Court's adherence to the metaphor as an analytical guide had led to inconsistent and unprincipled results in Establishment Clause cases. "Whether due to its lack of historical support of its practical unworkability," added Rehnquist, "the *Everson* 'wall' has proven all but useless as a guide to sound constitutional adjudication."[52] He then alluded to the wisdom of Justice Benjamin Cardozo's observation that "metaphors in law are to be narrowly watched, for starting as devices to liberate thought, they end often by enslaving it."[53]

"But the greatest injury of the 'wall' notion," Rehnquist argued, "is its mischievous diversion of judges from the actual intentions of the drafters of the Bill of Rights."[54] Rehnquist concluded his assault on the metaphor with a poignant recommendation: "The 'wall of separation between church and State' is a metaphor based on bad history, a metaphor which has proved useless as a guide to judging. It should be frankly and explicitly abandoned."[55]

The question of whether Rehnquist's recommendation should be taken seriously is, of course, dependent on whether his reading of the intentions of the drafters of the religion clauses is accurate or flawed. Fortunately, Rehnquist provided in the *Jaffree* case a summary of his interpretation of the framers' intentions, at least insofar as they are discoverable from the proceedings of the First Congress, and that interpretation can now be examined.

---

51. Ibid., 2516-17.

52. Ibid., 2517.

53. Ibid. The Cardozo quotation is from *Berkey* v. *Third Avenue R. Co.*, 155 N.E. 58 (1926), 61.

54. Ibid., 2517.

55. Ibid.

Rehnquist's Interpretation of the Proceedings of the First Congress

The 1985 *Jaffree* case is the only Supreme Court case in which William Rehnquist has discussed his views on the proceedings of the First Congress and on the intent of the framers who fashioned the religion clauses in those proceedings. In his dissenting opinion in *Jaffree*, Rehnquist did not review in detail the proceedings that led to the adoption of the religion clauses. He focused on only what he considered to be the relevant, dispositive portions of those proceedings, beginning by referring to the opening session of 8 June 1789, when James Madison proposed for House approval a series of amendments to the Constitution.

It will be remembered from the previous chapter that Madison's proposed amendment on religion read: "The civil rights of none shall be abridged on account of religious belief or worship, nor shall any national religion be established, nor shall the full and equal rights of conscience be in any manner, or any pretext, infringed."[56] The amendment, with the other amendments that were to form the Bill of Rights, was referred by the House to a committee of the whole, and after several weeks' delay was then referred to a Select Committee consisting of Madison and ten others. The Committee revised Madison's proposed amendment on religion to read: "No religion shall be established by law, nor shall the equal rights of conscience be infringed."[57]

Rehnquist noted that the Committee's proposed revisions were debated in the House on 15 August 1789. Rehnquist then offered an abbreviated account of the debate on the religion clauses as it appears in the *Annals*.[58] Because Rehnquist is somewhat reliant on certain portions of the debate, and because the full report of the debate in the *Annals* is not lengthy, it is given in full here. It is important to note, however, that the account of the debate, as reported in the *Annals*, is a condensed and paraphrased version rather than a verbatim report.

---

56. *Annals*, 1:451, quoted in ibid., 2510.
57. Ibid., 1:757, quoted in 105 S. Ct. 2479 (1985), 2510.
58. 105 S. Ct. 2479 (1985), 2510-12.

Saturday, August 15 [1789]

AMENDMENT TO THE CONSTITUTION

The House again went into a Committee of the Whole on the proposed amendments to the constitution. Mr. Boudinot in the chair.

The fourth proposition being under consideration, as follows:

Article 1. Section 9. Between paragraphs two and three insert "no religion shall be established by law, nor shall the equal rights of conscience be infringed."

Mr. Sylvester had some doubts of the propriety of the mode of expression used in this paragraph. He apprehended that it was liable to a construction different from what had been made by the committee. He feared it might be thought to have a tendency to abolish religion altogether.

Mr. Vining suggested the propriety of transposing the two members of the sentence.

Mr. Gerry said it would read better if it was, that no religious doctrine shall be established by law.

Mr. Sherman thought the amendment altogether unnecessary, inasmuch as Congress had no authority whatever delegated to them by the constitution to make religious establishments; he would, therefore, move to have it struck out.

Mr. Carroll.—As the rights of conscience are, in their nature, of peculiar delicacy, and will little bear the gentlest touch of governmental hand; and as many sects have concurred in opinion that they are not well secured under the present constitution, he said he was much in favor of adopting the words. He thought it would tend more towards conciliating the minds of the people to the Government than almost any other amendment he had heard proposed. He would not contend with gentlemen about the phraseology, his object was to secure the substance in such a manner as to satisfy the wishes of the honest part of the community.

Mr. Madison said, he apprehended the meaning of the words to be, that Congress should not establish a religion, and enforce the legal observation of it by law, nor compel men to worship

God in any manner contrary to their conscience. Whether the words are necessary or not, he did not mean to say, but they had been required by some of the State Conventions, who seemed to entertain an option that under the clause of the constitution, which gave power to Congress to make all laws necessary and proper to carry into execution the constitution, and the laws made under it, enabled them to make laws of such a nature as might infringe the rights of conscience, and establish a national religion; to prevent these effects he presumed the amendment was intended, and he thought it as well expressed as the nature of the language would admit.

Mr. Huntington said that he feared, with the gentleman first up on this subject, that the words might be taken in such latitude as to be extremely hurtful to the cause of religion. He understood the amendment to mean what had been expressed by the gentleman from Virginia; but others might find it convenient to put another construction upon it. The ministers of their congregations to the Eastward were maintained by the contributions of those who belonged to their society; the expense of building meeting-houses was contributed in the same manner. These things were regulated by by-laws. If an action was brought before a Federal Court on any of these cases, the person who had neglected to perform his engagements could not be compelled to do it; for a support of ministers, or building places of worship might be construed into a religious establishment.

By the charter of Rhode Island, no religion could be established by law; he could give a history of the effects of such a regulation; indeed the people were now enjoying the blessed fruits of it. [Intended as irony.] He hoped, therefore, the amendment would be made in such a way as to secure the rights of conscience, and a free exercise of the rights of religion, but not to patronize those who professed no religion at all.

Mr. Madison thought, if the word national was inserted before religion, it would satisfy the minds of honorable gentlemen. He believed that the people feared one sect might obtain a pre-eminence, or two combine together, and establish a religion to which they would compel others to conform. He thought if the word national was introduced, it would point the amendment directly to the object it was intended to prevent.

Mr. Livermore was not satisfied with that amendment; but he did not wish them to dwell long on the subject. He thought it would be better if it was altered, and made to read in this manner, that Congress shall make no laws touching religion, or infringing the rights of conscience.

Mr. Gerry did not like the term national, proposed by the gentleman from Virginia, and he hoped it would not be adopted by the House. It brought to his mind some observations that had taken place in the conventions at the time they were considering the present constitution. It had been insisted upon by those who were called anti-federalists, that this form of Government consolidated the Union; the honorable gentleman's motion shows that he considers it in the same light. Those who were called antifederalists at that time complained that they had injustice done them by the title, because they were in favor of a Federal Government, and the others were in favor of a national one; the federalists were for ratifying the constitution as it stood, and the others not until amendments were made. Their names then ought not to have been distinguished by federalists and antifederalists, but rats and antirats.

Mr. Madison withdrew his motion, but observed that the words "No national religion shall be established by law," did not imply that the Government was a national one; the question was then taken on Mr. Livermore's motion, and passed in the affirmative, thirty-one for, and twenty against it.[59]

Rehnquist then proceeded in his *Jaffree* dissent to give a brief chronology of the events leading to the passage of the religion clauses: (1) the House altered slightly the Committee's wording; (2) the Senate debated the Amendment in secret, of which there is no record; (3) the Senate's final proposal was submitted to the House but rejected; and (4) a joint House-Senate committee was formed that was able to agree upon the language later formally approved by the House and Senate: "Congress shall make no law respecting an establishment of religion or prohibiting the free exercise thereof."[60]

---

59. *Annals*, 1:1757-59; reprinted in Kurland and Lerner, *The Founder's Constitution*, 5: Amendment 1 (Religion), No. 53, pp. 72-74.

60. 105 S. Ct. 2479 (1985), 2511-12 (Rehnquist, J., dissenting).

On the basis of the record of these proceedings, Rehnquist stated his belief that Madison was undoubtedly the most important architect of the Bill of Rights among the members of the House of Representatives, but "as an advocate of sensible legislative compromise, not as an advocate of incorporating the Virginia Statute of Religious Freedom into the United States Constitution."[61]

Rehnquist then proceeded to give the heart of his argument for a narrow interpretation of the Establishment Clause in the following remarks:

> During the ratification debate in the Virginia Convention, Madison had actually opposed the idea of any Bill of Rights. His sponsorship of the amendments in the House was obviously not that of a zealous believer in the necessity of the Religion Clauses, but of one who felt it might do some good, could do no harm, and would satisfy those who had ratified the Constitution on the condition that Congress propose a Bill of Rights. His original language "nor shall any national religion be established" obviously does not conform to the "wall of separation" between church and State idea which latter day commentators have ascribed to him. His explanation on the floor of the meaning of his language—"that Congress should not establish a religion, and enforce the legal observation of it by law" is of the same ilk. When he replied to Huntington in the debate over the proposal which came from the Select Committee of the House, he urged that the language "no religion shall be established by law" should be amended by inserting the word "national" in front of the word "religion."
>
> It seems indisputable from these glimpses of Madison's thinking, as reflected by actions on the floor of the House in 1789, that he saw the amendment as designed to prohibit the establishment of a national religion, and perhaps to prevent discrimination among sects. He did not see it as requiring neutrality on the part of government between religion and irreligion.[62]

On this interpretation, then, Rehnquist argued that the Court's opinion in *Everson,* while correct in bracketing Jefferson and Madison

---

61. Ibid., 2512.
62. Ibid.

together in their exertions in their home state leading to the "Virginia Statute of Religious Freedom," is totally incorrect in suggesting that Madison carried these same views to the First Congress when he proposed the amendments that would ultimately become, in modified form, the Bill of Rights.[63] Moreover, Rehnquist suggested, the *Everson* error was repeated in *McCollum* v. *Board of Education*,[64] *Engel* v. *Vitale*,[65] and *Abington School District* v. *Schempp*.[66] He added that in *Schempp* the Court "made the truly remarkable statement that 'the views of Madison and Jefferson preceded by Roger Williams came to be incorporated . . . in the Federal Constitution. . . .' "[67]

Finally, on the basis of the marshaled evidence, Rehnquist concluded that the Court's reading of history was badly mistaken. He again referred to the proceedings of the First Congress, noting that the only concern of those who had spoken in the debates seemed "to have been the establishment of a national church, and perhaps the preference of one religious sect over another. . . ."[68]

In analyzing Rehnquist's argument, it is apparent that one major difference between Rehnquist and the Court majorities who decided for a broad interpretation of the Establishment Clause in *Everson*, *McCollum*, *Engel*, and *Schempp* is that Rehnquist believes that the Establishment Clause should be understood strictly on the basis of the words contained in the clause and the congressional proceedings that produced them, whereas those justices who have opted for the broad interpretation believe that sources outside of the words of the Establishment Clause and the congressional proceedings that produced them should be consulted. Rehnquist emphasizes the congressional debates, especially Madison's participation, in ascertaining the meaning of the clause. Those justices who have interpreted the clause broadly have generally sought to examine the history that led up to the congressional proceedings—and especially the important battle for religious

---

63. Ibid.
64. 333 U.S. 203 (1948).
65. 370 U.S. 421 (1963).
66. 374 U.S. 203 (1963).
67. 105 S. Ct. 2479 (1985), 2512 (Rehnquist, J., dissenting), quoting *Schempp*, 374 U.S. 203 (1963), 214.
68. Ibid., 2513.

liberty in Virginia led by Jefferson and Madison—in ascertaining the meaning of the clause.

Rehnquist is correct in asserting that the Court in *Everson*, *McCollum*, *Engel*, and *Schempp* relied heavily upon the experience of Jefferson and Madison in Virginia. In doing so, the Court in those cases formed the view that the religious liberty being fought for in the States—recognizing that Virginia was the leader in defining the meaning of religious liberty—had multiple dimensions, and that the Establishment Clause, as finally adopted, meant more than, if only implicitly, the mere prohibition against a national church or the discrimination among sects. The "Virginia Statute for Religious Freedom," for example, cited and relied upon by the Court in arriving at a broad interpretation of the Establishment Clause in *Everson*, *Engel*, and *Schempp*, specifies various improper governmental acts (arguably, "establishments"), including the influencing of religious belief by civil coercion, requiring men to support financially religious opinions they abhor, prohibiting men from holding office unless they profess certain religious beliefs, and incarcerating men for their religious opinions (see Appendix A).

Rehnquist, however, rejects the notion that the kinds of prohibitions enumerated in the Virginia Statute were embodied in the religion clauses, except to the extent they might be covered by the governmental restraints against interfering with the free exercise of religion. For Rehnquist, the prohibition against "an establishment of religion" contained in the First Amendment is limited in meaning primarily to that which was discussed in the proceedings of the First Congress. His view is that the framers were not seeking to duplicate that which was done in Virginia, or in any of the other states, for the advancement of religious liberty; the scope of the congressional proceedings was more limited in that they were only concerned that the new central government not be permitted to create a national church or discriminate among sects in the support of religion.

The approach of William Rehnquist in ascertaining the original intent of the framers is an application of his strict constructionism. It is a commitment to the meaning of the "words" in the religion clauses, aided almost exclusively in the interpretation of the meaning of the "words" by the immediate proceedings that produced the words. Rehnquist's approach is certainly not to be condemned on its face; it merely leads to conclusions about the meanings of the religion clauses that are *different* from conclusions reached by those who are not as committed to strict constructionism. By methodology, Rehnquist is systematically drawn to a narrow interpretation of the Establishment Clause; those with whom Rehnquist is so strongly in disagreement are systematically drawn to a broad interpretation by their methodology.

Even if sources outside of the congressional proceedings that produced the religion clauses are not consulted, there still remains the question of whether the religion clauses produced by those proceedings carry the meaning that Rehnquist says "seems indisputable."[69] Rehnquist's argument for his narrow interpretation of the Establishment Clause appeals to Madison's frequent references to a "national" religion. He cites three events: (1) the appearance of the language "nor shall any national religion be established" in Madison's first proposal; (2) Madison's explanation of the meaning of his language—"that Congress should not establish a religion, and enforce the legal observation of it by law"; and (3) Madison's statement to Huntington in floor debate urging that the language "no religion shall be established by law" should be amended by inserting the word "national" in front of the word "religion."

Rehnquist's argument is persuasive. However, as previously discussed, there still exists the possibility that Madison, by his use of the word "national" in all three events cited by Rehnquist, intended to distinguish an act of the national government from that of a state, without regard to the preferential or nonpreferential character of the national act on a matter respecting religion. In the floor debate, he may have suggested inserting the word "national" in front of the word "religion" to mean that "Congress should not establish a religion," which is, significantly, the very explanation that he offered when he first spoke in the debate to explain the meaning of the pending proposal on 15 August 1789: "No religion shall be established by law, nor shall equal rights of conscience be infringed."[70] On this interpretation,

---

69. Ibid., 2512.

70. See Madison's first remarks in the 15 August 1789 House debate, the full text of which appears above. The citation for the debate is given in footnote 59 above.

it seems that Madison may have discussed the clause as if the word "national" still appeared in it, yet he interpreted its meaning as prohibiting Congress from establishing a religion, not prohibiting Congress from establishing a "national" religion.[71]

That Madison meant merely a national church or no preference in the support of religion is also made questionable on the basis of Madison's attitude toward chaplaincies. In his "Detached Memoranda," Madison offered the following statement of his views on congressional chaplainships: "The Constitution of the U.S. forbids everything like an establishment of a national religion. The law appointing Chaplains establishes a religious worship for the national representatives, to be performed by ministers of religion . . . and these are to be paid out of the national taxes. Does this not involve the principle of a national establishment . . . ?"[72] Madison classified military chaplaincies "in the same way," as forbidden "establishments" or an "establishment of a national religion."[73]

Rehnquist's narrow interpretation of the Establishment Clause, as determined from the intent of the framers who participated in the First Congress, may be given historical support, but it cannot be established as correct by such a considerable reliance upon the input of James Madison. There is simply too much evidence that Madison believed that the Establishment Clause did more than prevent the creation of a national church or the favoring of one religion or sect over others.

Early National Accommodations of Religion

While William Rehnquist is reluctant to look historically beyond the proceedings of the First Congress to determine the precise meaning of the Establishment Clause, he is not hesitant to marshal post-1789 governmental acts as evidence that the 1789 framers intended only

---

71. See Levy, *The Establishment Clause*, 97-98.
72. Fleet, "Madison's Detached Memoranda," 554.
73. Ibid., 559-60.

to prohibit a national religion or the preference of one sect over another. There is no doubt that the early national government was sometimes less than timorous about permitting government acts that were mixed with religious overtones. The Northwest Ordinance and early presidential proclamations of prayer and thanksgiving were early governmental acts that, according to Rehnquist, indicate that the federal government never intended that it must always be neutral between religion and irreligion.

In 1787, operating under the Articles of Confederation, the United States passed the Northwest Ordinance. It was an important piece of legislation because it established the basic pattern for how the republic was to be geographically extended. Inhabitants of the territories would be United States citizens, and a territory could frame a constitution and apply for statehood when its population numbered 60,000 or more.[74] Obviously, potential inhabitants were concerned that they would enjoy the same civil and religious liberties they had enjoyed in the states. Thus, two significant provisions were included in the Ordinance. The first of these provisions was a guarantee of the free exercise of religion and stated that "no person, demeaning himself in a peaceable and orderly manner shall, ever be molested on account of his mode of worship, or religious sentiments, in the said territory."[75] A second provision in the Ordinance provided that "religion, morality, and knowledge being necessary to good government and the happiness of mankind, schools and the means of education shall forever be encouraged."[76] The Northwest Ordinance was reenacted by the First Congress on 7 August 1789.[77]

William Rehnquist, in his dissent in the *Jaffree* case, argued, in referring to the second of the two provisions quoted above, that the Northwest Ordinance confirms "the view that Congress did not mean that the government should be neutral between religion and irreli-

---

74. Richard N. Current, T. Harry Williams, and Frank Freidel, *American History: A Survey*, 2nd ed. (New York: Alfred A. Knopf, 1966), 125-26.)

75. United States Code 1:xlii (1976 Edition).

76. Ibid., xliii.

77. Public Statutes at Large, vol. 1, "First Congress, of the Territory Northwest of the River Ohio," 50.

gion."[78] Rehnquist noted that "it seems highly unlikely that the House of Representatives would simultaneously consider proposed amendments to the Constitution and enact an important piece of legislation which conflicted with the intent of the proposals."[79]

Quite literally, the Northwest Ordinance *is* an "establishment of religion" under the current Supreme Court's broad interpretation of the Establishment Clause. And, as Rehnquist noted, it does seem unlikely that the First Congress would have reenacted the Ordinance in 1789 if they thought it would violate the proposed Bill of Rights.

However, there are a number of facts that support the possibility that the framers may not have considered the Ordinance to be problematic. To begin with, the reenactment of the Ordinance took place on 7 August 1789, eight days before debates on the proposed religion clauses even began. The argument that Congress, in passing the Northwest Ordinance, did so in contravention of matters that it had not yet even discussed on the floor, is not convincing. In addition, the two provisions of the Ordinance dealing with religion may together have been understood by Congress simply to guarantee religious liberty in the territories. There was a prevailing sentiment in favor of religious freedom, and Congress may merely have considered itself to be acting to ensure that territorial settlers would enjoy religious freedom. Finally, a draft of the original Ordinance, considered two days before its passage by the Continental Congress in 1787, read as follows: "Institutions for the promotion of religion and morality, schools and the means of education shall forever be encouraged."[80] In the final version, the language calling for the encouragement of religious institutions was dropped in favor of the encouragement of schools and the means of education. This change could indicate that Congress was at least considering "establishment" overtones; they may have been attempting to ensure that the sustenance of religious life would come from the

---

78. 105 S. Ct. 2479 (1985), 2513.

79. Ibid. For discussions supporting this view, see John S. Baker, "James Madison and Religious Freedom," *Benchmark* 3 (January-April 1987): 71-78; and Robert L. Cord, *Separation of Church and State*, 61-62.

80. Quoted in Bernard Schwartz, *The Bill of Rights: A Documentary History* (New York: Chelsea House, 1971), 395.

people and the schools, not from government.[81]

In the final analysis, the relationship between the Northwest Ordinance and the intentions of the framers with regard to the separation of church and state is not clear. It is not surprising, therefore, that both separationists and accommodationists claim the Northwest Ordinance as supportive of their own views.

Rehnquist also sought confirmation for his version of the framers' understanding of the Establishment Clause in the early proclamations of days for thanksgiving and prayer. He noted that George Washington, John Adams, and James Madison all issued proclamations designating certain days for prayer and thanksgiving to God.[82] There can be little doubt that these traditions are evidence that some forms of public prayer were not believed to constitute an establishment of religion. Similar invocations have been used by Lincoln, Cleveland, Wilson, Roosevelt, Eisenhower, Kennedy,[83] and, more recently, Ronald Reagan. They are sure signs of the spiritual tradition that is part of the American culture.

In spite of the large number of presidents who have sanctioned official public prayers, at least two early presidents were not in favor of the practice. As Rehnquist himself noted, Jefferson opposed official prayer, believing that it was best left in the hands of the people, "where the Constitution had deposited it."[84]

James Madison also had reservations about the practice. In his "Detached Memoranda," Madison stated that "thanksgiving and fasts . . . seem to imply and certainly nourish the erroneous [sic] idea of a national religion."[85] He was apparently somewhat flexible on the matter, however, because he proclaimed several days for fasting and thanksgiving. He reportedly found extenuating circumstances in the fact that he was president during the time a war was fought on national soil.[86]

---

81. Ibid.
82. 105 S. Ct. 2479 (1985), 2514 (Rehnquist, J., dissenting).
83. *Engel* v. *Vitale,* 370 U.S. 421 (1962), 445 n. 3 (Stewart, J., dissenting).
84. 105 S. Ct. 2479 (1985), 2514 (Rehnquist, J., dissenting).
85. Fleet, "Madison's Detached Memoranda," 560.
86. Ibid.

The practices of government-sanctioned prayer are, by all admissions, a violation of a strict separation of church and state. They were violations in the early days of the republic and they remain so today. Yet they are elements of a "civil religion" deeply rooted in America's cultural traditions. They are likely to continue as practices favored by a large segment of a people who are, for the most part, keenly religious. Because religion can never be completely separated from people and their secular institutions, it is best that separationists and accommodationists alike make some allowance for prayer in a republic that does not seek to be hostile to religion. As proof that the framers intended to prohibit only a national church and preferential treatment of certain sects, however, public prayers by presidents are of some weight, but not very much.

Chapter 7

REHNQUIST, THE SUPREME COURT, AND THE QUEST FOR GUIDELINES IN APPLYING THE RELIGION CLAUSES

The *Lemon* Three-Part Test: "A Determined Effort to Craft a Workable Rule from an Historically Faulty Doctrine"

As noted earlier, in *Lemon* v. *Kurtzman* (1971),[1] the Supreme Court formally packaged a three-pronged test to serve as a set of guidelines in deciding Establishment Clause issues. The stated reason for the need for such a formal set of guidelines was the "opaque" language of the religion clauses, especially the word "respecting" appearing in the Establishment Clause.

In *Lemon*, the Court noted: "A law 'respecting' the proscribed result, that is, the establishment of religion, is not always easily identifiable as one violative of the Clause."[2] Writing for the Court, Chief Justice Burger explained that guidelines were needed to guard against the three main evils against which the Establishment Clause was intended to afford protection: "sponsorship, financial support, and active involvement of the sovereign in religious activity."[3] Burger further

---

1. 403 U.S. 602 (1971).
2. Ibid., 612.
3. Ibid. The quoted language was adopted by Chief Justice Burger from *Walz* v. *Tax Commission*, 397 U.S. 664 (1970), 668.

explained that the criteria were not new; they had developed over many years, and there had emerged three key tests. He then stated the three-part test: "First, the statute must have a secular legislative purpose; second, its principal or primary effect must be one that neither advances nor inhibits religion; finally, the statute must not foster an excessive government entanglement with religion."[4]

From 1971 (post-Lemon) to 1982, the Court's steadfast commitment to the Lemon test could be summarized by the Court's statement in Committee for Public Education v. Nyquist (1973):[5] "To pass muster under the Establishment Clause the law must conform to the test."[6] According to some, curious distinctions arose out of the cases during that period; one seeking to make sense out of the Court's rulings is, in A. E. Dick Howard's words, "in for a shock."[7] The Lemon test, applied to the cases during that twelve-year period, yielded what were, for many, inconsistent, if not sometimes bizarre, results.

Eventually, William Rehnquist was moved to give a rather caustic summary of the results of many of the cases:

> For example, a State may lend to parochial school children geography textbooks that contain maps of the United States, but the State may not lend maps of the United States for use in geography class. A State may lend textbooks on American colonial history, but it may not lend a film on George Washington, or a film projector to show it in history class. A state may lend classroom workbooks, but may not lend workbooks in which the parochial school children write, thus rendering them nonreusable. A State may pay for bus transportation to religious schools but may not pay for bus transportation from the parochial school to the public zoo or natural history museum for a field trip. A State may pay for diagnostic services conducted in the parochial school but therapeutic services must be given in a different building; speech and hearing "services"

---

4. Ibid. The "purpose" and "effect" tests are usually traced to Abington School District v. Schempp, 374 U.S. 203 (1963), although some trace the "purpose" test to the earlier case of McGowan v. Maryland, 396 U.S. (1961). The "entanglement" test originated in Walz v. Tax Commission; ibid.

5. 413 U.S. 756 (1973).

6. Ibid., 772-73 (emphasis added).

7. Howard, "The Wall of Separation," 95.

conducted by the State inside the sectarian school are forbidden, but the State may conduct speech and hearing diagnostic testing inside the sectarian school. Exceptional parochial school students may receive counseling, but it must take place outside of the parochial school, such as in a trailer parked down the street. A State may give cash to a parochial school to pay for the administration of State written tests and state ordered reporting services, but it may not provide funds for teacher-prepared tests on secular subjects. Religious instruction may not be given in public school, but the public school may release students during the day for religion classes elsewhere, and may enforce attendance at those classes with its truancy laws.[8]

In analyzing the reasons for the problems created by the *Lemon* test, Rehnquist traced his way back to the early Establishment Clause cases—especially *Schempp*, which contained the "purpose" and "effect" tests. In his view, the *Schempp* case suffered from the same malady as *Everson* and other early Establishment Clause cases: they were erro-

---

8. *Wallace* v. *Jaffree*, 105 S. Ct. 2479 (1985), 2518-19. The compendium of results offered by Rehnquist are found in the following cases: *Committee for Public Education* v. *Nyquist*, 413 U.S. 756 (1973); *Meek* v. *Pittenger*, 421 U.S. 349 (1975); *Wolman* v. *Walter*, 433 U.S. 229 (1977); *Zorach* v. *Clauson*, 343 U.S. 306 (1952); and *Board of Education* v. *Allen*, 392 U.S. 236 (1968). The results summarized by Rehnquist do appear, upon initial consideration, quite bizarre. However, one author has offered a brief, yet dispassionate, appraisal in support of the Court's holdings. In J. W. Peltason, *Understanding the Constitution* (New York: Holt, Rinehart, and Winston, 1988), 139, the author comments: "If taxes can be used for textbooks, why not for teachers? If for standardized tests, why not for teacher-prepared tests? If for transportation to school, why not for transportation on field trips? If for books, why not for maps? If for counseling outside a parochial school, why not inside? 'A textbook is ascertainable,' but a teacher's handling of a subject is not. A standardized test is not prepared by church schools, but teacher-prepared tests are an 'integral part of the teaching process.' Transportation to and from school is a routine round trip every student makes every day and is unrelated to any aspect of the curriculum; field trips are controlled by teachers and are an aid to instructional programs. Counseling outside a school is less likely to involve religious matters than is counseling within the 'pervasively sectarian atmosphere of the school.' As for its approval of tax-purchased books but disapproval of tax-purchased records, maps, and other kinds of instructional materials, the Court has recognized there is a 'tension' between its holdings. Nonetheless, the judges argue, when a standardized textbook is used both in public and church-operated schools, it provides assurance that the books will not be sectarian or used for sectarian purposes, whereas there is much greater danger that other kinds of teaching materials may be diverted to religious purposes."

neously decided on the "wall of separation" theory. The connection between the post-*Lemon* cases and *Schempp* was obvious for Rehnquist: "the purpose and effect prongs have the same historical deficiencies as the wall concept itself: *they are in no way based on either the language or intent of the drafters.*"[9] He continued, "The three-part test represents a determined effort to craft a workable rule from an historically faulty doctrine; but the rule can only be as sound as the doctrine it attempts to service."[10]

Before Rehnquist's assault on the *Lemon* test in *Jaffree*, the Supreme Court had already begun wavering on the *Lemon* guidelines. In *Marsh v. Chambers* (1983),[11] which upheld Nebraska's longstanding practice of paying a chaplain to open legislative sessions, the Court did not even mention the three-part test. Rather, an argument from history, emphasizing the rich tradition of chaplaincies, was emphasized in finding the Nebraska practice constitutional.

In *Mueller v. Allen* (1983),[12] the three-part test was utilized to reach a decision, but probably more out of formality than commitment. The Court upheld a Minnesota statute allowing income tax deductions for tuition, textbooks, and transportation of dependents, reasoning that the deductions were available to all parents, whether their children attended public, private, or church-related schools.[13] Writing for the Court, Justice Rehnquist downplayed the three-part test: "While this principle is well settled, our cases have also emphasized that it provides 'no more than [a] helpful signpost' in dealing with Establishment Clause challenges."[14]

In *Lynch v. Donnelly* (1984),[15] the Court refused to prohibit the City of Pawtucket, Rhode Island, from erecting an elaborate Christmas

---

9. 105 S. Ct. 2479 (1985), 2517 (emphasis added).

10. Ibid., 2518.

11. 463 U.S. 783 (1983).

12. 463 U.S. 388 (1983).

13. The *Mueller* case was distinguished from the Court's holding in *Committee for Public Education* v. *Nyquist*, 413 U.S. 756 (1973), where a New York statute was struck down because it permitted income tax deductions *only* for parents sending their dependents to parochial schools, thus failing the "purpose" test.

14. 463 U.S. 388 (1983), 394, quoting *Hunt* v. *McNair*, 413 U.S. 734 (1973), 741.

15. 465 U.S. 668 (1984).

display that included a life-sized crèche. In writing the Court's majority opinion, Chief Justice Burger asserted that "we have repeatedly emphasized our unwillingness to be confined to any single test or criterion in this sensitive area."[16] Burger then cited two cases, *Marsh* and *Larson* v. *Valente* (1982),[17] in which the Court had failed to find the *Lemon* three-part test useful. Moreover, Justice O'Connor, in a concurring opinion in *Lynch*, suggested a redefinition of the *Lemon* test, in which the purpose and effect prongs would prohibit government "endorsement" or "disapproval" of religion—that is, when a law makes adherence to religion relevant to a person's standing in the political community. She repeated this view in *Jaffree*, *Aguilar* v. *Felton*,[18] and *Latter-Day Saints* v. *Amos*.[19]

Other justices have also expressed dissatisfaction with the three-part test. While he concurred with the Court's ruling in *Roemer* v. *Board of Public Works of Maryland* (1976),[20] Justice Byron White voiced his displeasure with the entanglement test, which he found "curious and mystifying."[21]

Justice John Paul Stevens is another critic of the Court's three-part test, despite the fact that he usually reaches separationist results, which the *Lemon* test favors. In *Wolman* v. *Walter* (1977),[22] Stevens opined that the Court, having failed to improve on the "no tax support to religion" test of *Everson*, had simply encouraged the states "to search for new ways of achieving forbidden ends."[23] Stevens seemed to suggest scrapping the three-part test altogether and returning to the *Everson* standard. Yet, in writing the Court's opinion in *Jaffree*, Stevens employed the three-part test but used language that seemed to endorse Justice O'Connor's concept that the purpose prong is violated if the statute in question "endorses" religion.

Examined as a group, the cases after 1982 indicate that the justices

---

16. Ibid., 679.
17. 456 U.S. 228 (1982).
18. 105 S. Ct. 3232 (1985) (O'Connor, J., dissenting).
19. 107 S. Ct. 2862 (1987) (O'Connor, J., dissenting).
20. 426 U.S. 736 (1976).
21. Ibid., 768 (White, J., concurring).
22. 433 U.S. 229 (1977).
23. Ibid., 265 (Stevens, J., concurring in part and dissenting in part).

are becoming increasingly unsettled with the *Lemon* three-part test.[24] Yet the three-part test continues to be utilized, and only William Rehnquist has called for a total abandonment of the *Lemon* criteria. He summarized his sentiments concerning the three-part test in his *Jaffree* dissent: "If a constitutional theory has no basis in the history of the amendment it seeks to interpret, is difficult to apply and yields unprincipled results, I see little use in it."[25]

If Rehnquist could replace the *Lemon* three-part test, what would he replace it with? He has never offered a comprehensive statement of what kind of legislation would not violate Establishment Clause standards. He usually has defined the Establishment Clause in terms of what it prohibits: (1) "the designation of any church as a 'national' one,"[26] and (2) the preference by "the federal government for one religious denomination or sect over others."[27] These prohibitions are, of course, expressed in relation to the original intent of the framers— before "incorporation." Having apparently "given in" to incorporation,[28] these same prohibitions would now apply to the states.

However, we do have from Rehnquist, by way of application of Establishment Clause principles to various factual settings, a number of statements that aid in shaping the contours of what, for Rehnquist, the Clause permits or prohibits. The Establishment Clause, for example, prohibits "government support of proselytizing activities of religious sects by throwing the weight of secular authorities behind the dissemination of religious tenets."[29] Neither will the clause permit "purposeful assistance directly to the church itself or to some religious group . . . performing ecclesiastical functions."[30] The clause permits "governmental assistance which does not have the effect of 'inducing'

---

24. In *Edwards* v. *Aquillard*, 107 S. Ct. 2573 (1987), Justice Antonin Scalia joined the ranks of justices who doubt the usefulness of the *Lemon* test.

25. 105 S. Ct. 2479 (1985), 2519 (Rehnquist, J., dissenting).

26. Ibid., 2520.

27. Ibid.

28. Ibid.

29. *Thomas* v. *Review Board of Indiana Employment Security Division*, 450 U.S. 707 (1981), 726 (Rehnquist, J., dissenting), quoting Justice Stewart in his dissent in *Abington School District* v. *Schempp*, 374 U.S. 203 (1963), 314.

30. Ibid., quoting Justice Reed in his dissent in *McCollum* v. *Board of Education*, 333 U.S. 203 (1948), 248.

religious belief but merely 'accommodates' or implements an independent religious choice."[31] The clause "does not prohibit Congress or the States from pursuing legitimate secular ends through nondiscriminatory sectarian means."[32] And, lastly, the clause "does not forbid governments . . . to [provide] general welfare under which benefits are distributed to private individuals, even though many of those individuals may elect to use those benefits in ways that 'aid' religious instruction or worship."[33]

These statements define the approximate boundaries of Rehnquist's Establishment Clause. The boundaries are broad and leave a large area of acceptable governmental interaction with religion. Perhaps a summary statement of the level of permissible government involvement in religion, for Rehnquist, would be, roughly: any governmental assistance, whether to individuals or religious groups, which accommodates religious belief without preference, is constitutionally permissible.

The Tension Between Establishment and Free Exercise

Prohibiting an establishment of religion and securing the free exercise of religion are two ways of attaining a common goal—religious liberty. Neither Jefferson nor Madison considered the fight for religious liberty in Virginia complete until both rights were secure. It was natural, therefore, that the First Amendment contain both an establishment and a free exercise clause.[34]

The Supreme Court has, in the main, tended to view the religion clauses as embodying two separate mandates. Consequently, it has developed separate tests for determining whether government action violates either clause. The test for the Establishment Clause is the *Lemon* three-part test.

As for the Free Exercise Clause, the Court has said that if the

---

31. *Thomas* v. *Review Board of Indiana Employment Security Division*, 450 U.S. 707 (1981), 727 (Rehnquist, J., dissenting).

32. *Wallace* v. *Jaffree*, 105 S. Ct. 2479 (1985), 2520 (Rehnquist, J., dissenting).

33. Ibid., 2519.

34. Howard, "The Wall of Separation," 100-01.

purpose of a law "is to impede the observance of one or all religions, that law is constitutionally invalid."[35] Few laws, however, single out religion for adverse treatment. Most issues under the Free Exercise Clause arise when a government regulation, undertaken for genuinely secular purposes, penalizes or burdens conduct arising out of religious belief. In order to deal with this conflict between state interest and religious belief, the Supreme Court has usually employed "a balancing process"[36] and ruled that if a government regulation burdens the exercise of religion, then in the absence of a compelling state interest "of the highest order"[37] government must accommodate the religious interest by granting it an exemption from state regulation.

Thus, there arises an "ineluctable tension"[38] between the two provisions of the First Amendment. On the one hand, the Court has said that the Establishment Clause forbids government action when the purpose is to aid religion, but, on the other hand, the Court has said that the Free Exercise Clause may require government action to accommodate religion. In *Walz*, Chief Justice Burger conceded that the religion clauses "are cast in absolute terms, and either . . . , if expanded to a logical extreme, would tend to clash with the other."[39]

In its efforts to resolve the inevitable tensions that exist between the religion clauses, the Court has usually sought to maintain an attitude of neutrality, neither advancing nor inhibiting religion. Justice Hugo Black first appealed to the "neutrality" theme in *Everson* when he said that the First Amendment "requires the state to be neutral in its relations with groups of religious believers and non-believers."[40] Among the justices, Warren Burger was the most active spokesman for neutrality—or, as he preferred, "benevolent neutrality." Cautioning against the tendency toward "absolutist" readings of the First Amendment in earlier cases, Burger in *Walz* argued for "play in the joints productive of a benevolent neutrality which will permit religious

---

35. *Braunfeld v. Brown*, 366 U.S. 599 (1961), 607.
36. *Wisconsin v. Yoder*, 406 U.S. 205 (1972), 214.
37. Ibid., 215.
38. Choper, "The Religion Clauses," 673.
39. *Walz v. Tax Commission*, 397 U.S. 664 (1970), 668-69.
40. *Everson v. Board of Education*, 330 U.S. 1 (1947), 18.

exercise to exist without sponsorship and without interference."[41]

The *Walz* and *Wisconsin* v. *Yoder*[42] cases are perhaps best illustrative of the conflict between the religion clauses. In *Walz*, a taxpayer challenged a New York statute that provided tax exemptions for churches and other charitable groups. The taxpayer claimed that, because the churches in New York City were tax-exempt, he, as a taxpayer, was required financially to support the city's churches. The Court upheld the tax exemption despite the argument that it was a subsidy to the churches and thus amounted to a religious establishment. The exemption clearly treated property owned by churches differently from other property, but the Court upheld the exemption because taxation would have presented serious free exercise problems. In *Walz*, free exercise claims won out over establishment concerns.

Likewise, in *Yoder*, the Court restricted the state's power to require compulsory education of Amish children through age sixteen, citing the conflict with the religious interest of the Amish in educating their own school-age children. Balancing between legitimate state and private religious interests, the Court ruled in favor of a religious exemption for the Amish from the Wisconsin education laws. *Walz* and *Yoder* illustrate the tension inherent in the religion clauses. Neither clause can be read as an absolute because an absolute interpretation of either clause would ultimately swallow the other.

A number of scholars have argued that the Establishment Clause is designed to implement the Free Exercise Clause so that, when the two clauses clash, the Establishment Clause must be subordinated to the Free Exercise Clause.[43] The Supreme Court has never officially adopted this view although it may naturally appear that way when free exercise claims are given priority over establishment claims.[44] The Court has instead (at least until the 1990 case of *Employment Division of Oregon* v. *Smith*, discussed below) chosen the path of "neutrality,"

---

41. *Walz* v. *Tax Commission*, 397 U.S. 664 (1970), 669.

42. 406 U.S. 205 (1972).

43. See, for example, John Norton Moore, "The Supreme Court and the Relationship Between the 'Establishment' and 'Free Exercise' Clauses," *Texas Law Review* 42 (December 1963): 196; also, Van Patten, "The Meaning of the Religion Clauses," 87.

44. See, for example, *Sherbert* v. *Verner*, 374 U.S. 398 (1963).

seeking to accommodate religious belief, when possible, without advancing or sponsoring religion. Thus the Court's approach frequently has been less systematic than pragmatic, less committed to first principles than to reconciling decisions with prior decisions. As one writer has said, "The years since *Everson* have brought so much gloss on the First Amendment that the Court has fallen into the habit . . . of putting gloss on gloss."[45] A commitment to a vague "neutrality" only forces a case-by-case approach, and that has brought criticism from many on and off the Court. Chief among the critics on the Court has been William Rehnquist.

Rehnquist proposed his solution to the problem of the "tension" in the religion clauses in the case of *Thomas* v. *Review Board of Indiana Employment Security Division*.[46] In that case, as already noted, the Supreme Court required the State of Indiana to pay unemployment compensation to a Jehovah's Witness who quit his job for religious reasons after being transferred by his employer to a department that made turrets for military tanks. The Court upheld the worker's free exercise claim, held that there was no establishment of religion in doing so, and justified its holding on the basis of "neutrality in the face of religious differences."[47] Rehnquist dissented, complaining that the decision "adds mud to the already muddied waters of First Amendment jurisprudence."[48]

For Rehnquist, the Court's ruling was wrong for fundamental reasons:

> The decision today illustrates how far astray the Court has gone in interpreting the Free Exercise and Establishment Clauses of the First Amendment. Although the Court holds that a State is constitutionally required to provide direct financial assistance to persons solely on the basis of their religious beliefs and recognizes the "tension" between the two clauses, it does little to help resolve that tension. . . . Instead it simply asserts that there is no Establishment Clause violation here and leaves tension between the two

45. Howard, "The Wall of Separation," 113.
46. 450 U.S. 707 (1981).
47. Ibid., 720.
48. Ibid. (Rehnquist, J., dissenting).

Religion Clauses to be resolved on a case-by-case basis. . . . I believe that the "tension" is largely of this Court's own making, and would diminish almost to the vanishing point if the clauses were properly interpreted.[49]

Regarding the Free Exercise Clause, Rehnquist found no violation because the state of Indiana, in the interest of legitimate secular goals, had enacted an unemployment statute that provided no exemptions for religious reasons. Thomas was not singled out in the statute and there was no reason for the Court now to single him out for special exemption. The state had the right to make its own judgments, according to Rehnquist, about the kinds of exemptions, if any, it would grant.

As to the Establishment Clause issue, Rehnquist was quizzical as to why the Court had not applied the *Lemon* test to the facts of the case. "If Indiana were to legislate what the Court today requires—an unemployment law which permits benefits to be granted to those persons who quit their job for religious reasons—the statute would plainly violate the Establishment Clause. . . ."[50]

Finding no fault with the Court's approach under both of the religion clauses, Rehnquist stated his view of the proper approach: "If the Court were to construe the Free Exercise Clause as it did in *Braunfeld* and the Establishment Clause as Justice Stewart did [in dissent] in *Schempp,* the circumstances in which there would be a conflict between the two clauses would be few and far between."[51] In view of the Rehnquist designation of these two "model" approaches, a brief look at those opinions may aid in the goal of discovering Rehnquist's own solution to the "tension" between the religion clauses. The investigation of Rehnquist's solution is important also from the standpoint of seeing its apparent influence upon his fellow Court justices, who in the 1990 case of *Employment Division of Oregon* v. *Smith,* seemingly adopted Rehnquist's approach to dealing with free exercise claims.

In *Braunfeld* v. *Brown,*[52] Orthodox Jewish merchants had claimed

---

49. Ibid., 722.
50. Ibid., 723.
51. Ibid., 727.
52. 366 U.S. 599 (1961).

that, as a result of their own Saturday Sabbath observance and the state's Sunday closing laws, they were able to work only five days, thus placing them at great economic disadvantage. The Court upheld the Sunday closing laws and held that the indirect burden on the merchant's religious free exercise rights was not unreasonable. Rehnquist considered the holding to be a model for adjudicating free exercise claims—the state had valid secular reasons in having a compulsory Sunday closing law, and the law was essentially nondiscriminatory in its purposes and effects. The imposition on the Jewish merchants, much like the imposition on the Jehovah's Witness factory worker in *Thomas,* was unfortunate but did not mandate the carving out of religious exemptions when the state deemed it unnecessary.

In *Abington School District* v. *Schempp,*[53] Justice Stewart dissented from the Court's disallowance of Bible reading and recitals of the Lord's Prayer as daily exercises in the public school classrooms. The Court majority found that the statutes requiring the practices had no "secular purpose" and that their "primary effect" was the advancement of religion, both violations of the Establishment Clause. Stewart's view was that the Establishment Clause was violated only if there was active governmental support of religious sects by "throwing the weight of secular authorities behind the dissemination of religious tenets."[54] This approach found favor with Rehnquist because it permits government support of religion insofar as it is nondiscriminatory.

In uncovering Rehnquist's views from the *Braunfeld* case and Stewart's *Schempp* dissent, it becomes apparent that Rehnquist is simply calling for a narrower interpretation of both the Establishment Clause and the Free Exercise Clause. It is an approach in which governmental authority may legislate aid to religion without violating the Establishment Clause, provided the aid is granted nonpreferentially or there is a valid secular purpose behind the legislation. Any resulting conflicts with free exercise claims are more likely to be resolved in favor of the governmental authority than under the Court's usual "neutral" approach. The Court's neutral approach, still closer to the strict sepa-

---

53. 374 U.S. 203 (1963).
54. Ibid., 314 (Stewart, J., dissenting).

rationism of *Everson* than to the accommodationism of *Zorach*, is highly sensitive to any advancement of religion (establishment violation) or discrimination against religious minorities (free exercise violation). The sensitivity to these violations would be reduced under Rehnquist's approach, thus reducing the "tension" between the clauses.

The Court majority has usually erred, according to Rehnquist, in consistently giving an "overly expansive interpretation of *both* clauses."[55] In closing out his dissent in *Thomas*, Rehnquist's appeal was once again to the original intent of the framers, from which the Court, he deemed, had surely strayed: "Although I heartily agree with the Court's tacit abandonment of much of our rhetoric about the Establishment Clause, I regret that the Court cannot see its way clear to restore what was surely intended to have been a greater degree of flexibility to the federal and state governments in legislating consistently with the Free Exercise Clause."[56]

Nine years after the 1981 *Thomas* decision, Rehnquist's line of reasoning seemingly finally won out in the landmark case of *Employment Division of Oregon* v. *Smith*.[57] While the case did not explicitly deal with the tension between the religion clauses, and while Rehnquist did not write either the majority or a concurring opinion, he voted with the Court's majority in adopting an approach to adjudicating free exercise claims that bears a striking resemblance to Rehnquist's approach as presented in his *Thomas* dissent. Not coincidentally, of course, if the *Smith* case becomes entrenched as the Supreme Court's method of dealing with free exercise claims, it will have the effect of reducing the tension between the two religion clauses in the way that Rehnquist finds fitting.

Like the *Thomas* case, *Smith* involved an unemployment controversy. In 1984, Alfred Smith, a Klamath Indian, and Galen Black, a non-Indian, were fired from their jobs as drug counselors after the agency they worked for learned the pair had used the drug peyote during ceremonies in the Native American Church. Their employer,

---

55. *Thomas* v. *Review Board of Indiana Employment Division*, 450 U.S. 707 (1981), 721 (Rehnquist, J., dissenting) (emphasis in original).
56. Ibid., 726.
57. 110 S. Ct. 1595 (1990).

the Council on Alcohol and Drug Abuse Prevention Treatment (ADAPT), acted upon their stated policy, which was that all employees must be drug free. Smith and Black thought an exemption should be carved out for their religious use of peyote, a mild hallucinogen derived from cactus. For many Indians, peyote is revered as a gift from God or as the Comforter Jesus promised to send. Its sacramental ingestion is believed to teach humility, facilitate healing, and open paths of communication to God. ADAPT officials denied their request for a religious exemption, however, and both men were dismissed.

Smith and Black applied for unemployment benefits, but were turned down. The Employment Division of the Oregon Department of Human Resources ruled that the two had been fired for misconduct and therefore did not qualify for benefits. Smith and Black subsequently filed suit in an Oregon state court claiming that the State of Oregon had denied their right to the free exercise of their religion. Four years later, the Oregon Supreme Court agreed, holding that the ceremonial use of peyote is protected by the First Amendment.

When presented to the United States Supreme Court, the case appeared to most observers to be a routine occasion for the Court to apply the Court's twenty-seven-year-old "compelling state interest" test, which, as already noted, grew out of the 1963 *Sherbert* v. *Verner* decision. That test said that government can restrict religious freedom only when it proves there is a compelling interest to do so and when there is no less intrusive alternative available to achieve the state's goals. If the Court had wanted to deny the free exercise claims of Smith and Black, they could have easily done so by merely holding that the State of Oregon had a compelling interest in limiting drug use. Instead, however, in holding that the plaintiff's free exercise claims were unwarranted, five of the Court's justices voted to overturn the compelling state interest test, marking an abrupt shift in Supreme Court free exercise jurisprudence.

The *Smith* ruling granted state governments broad new powers over religious practices. The Court replaced the *Sherbert* test with a much narrower one, holding that government may offer religiously based exemptions from generally applicable laws if it chooses, without being under a constitutional requirement to do so. Writing for the majority, Justice Antonin Scalia stated, "We have never held that an individual's religious beliefs excuse him from compliance with an otherwise valid law prohibiting conduct that the State is free to regulate."[58] The continued adherence to the compelling state interest test, said Scalia, "would create a private right to ignore generally applicable laws" and would be "courting anarchy."[59]

The ruling is highly troublesome to many constitutional scholars because it seems to offer minority religions little protection from state legislative enactments that infringe upon their religious practices. Scalia admitted that the ruling might place minority religions at the mercy of legislatures who enact statutes prohibiting certain religious practices but he excused this as "unavoidable."[60] "It may be fairly said," commented Scalia, "that leaving accommodation to the political process will place at a relative disadvantage those religious practices that are not widely engaged in; but that unavoidable consequence of democratic government must be preferred to a system in which each conscience is a law unto itself or in which judges weigh the social importance of all laws against the centrality of all religious beliefs."[61]

The alignment of justices in the case was somewhat unusual. As expected, Chief Justice Rehnquist and Justices Anthony Kennedy and Byron White joined Scalia in his majority opinion. The surprising fifth vote, however, came from Justice John Paul Stevens. Stevens is generally considered a member of the Court's liberal wing and has usually favored a strict separationist reading of the Establishment Clause. That he opted for such a narrow reading of the Free Exercise Clause was somewhat unexpected.

Justice Sandra Day O'Connor concurred in the *Smith* result, but wrote a separate dissent that accused the majority of dramatically departing from well-settled precepts of First Amendment religious liberty. "In my view, today's holding . . . appears unnecessary to resolve the question presented, and is incompatible with our nation's fundamental commitment to individual religious liberty."[62] O'Connor would have

---

58. Ibid., 1600.
59. Ibid., 1605.
60. Ibid., 1606.
61. Ibid.
62. Ibid.

retained the compelling state interest test while holding that the State of Oregon did indeed have a compelling state interest—the regulation of drugs—that would override the free exercise rights of Smith and Black.

Justice Harry Blackmun wrote a dissenting opinion, joined by fellow justices William Brennan and Thurgood Marshall. They expressed agreement with O'Connor's opinion in its criticism of the majority for abandoning the *Sherbert* test, but would have held that Oregon had not shown a compelling state interest sufficient to nullify the free exercise rights of Smith and Black. Blackmun accused the Court majority of engaging in a "wholesale overturning of settled law concerning the Religion Clauses of our Constitution."[63] He added, "I do not believe the Founders thought their dearly bought freedom from religious persecution a 'luxury,' but an essential element of liberty— and they could not have thought religious intolerance 'unavoidable,' for they drafted the Religion Clauses precisely in order to avoid that intolerance."[64]

Many Court-watchers have argued and will continue to argue that the most alarming feature of Scalia's majority opinion in *Smith* is the diminished stature accorded to religious liberty as a fundamental freedom. Scalia acknowledged that judicial exemptions from neutral laws have sometimes been granted for religious reasons, but he argued that such exemptions have usually been granted only in conjunction with another constitutional right—such as free speech."[65] Justice O'Connor disagreed, calling the free exercise of religion a "preferred constitutional activity," entitled to "heightened judicial scrutiny."[66] She argued that the *Sherbert* test was an altogether workable one, formulated to "strike sensible balances between religious liberty and competing state interest."[67]

Indeed, it can be argued that the *Smith* decision sidesteps what was surely one of the main purposes of the Bill of Rights: to protect

---

63. Ibid., 1616.
64. Ibid.
65. Ibid., 1601.
66. Ibid., 1612.
67. Ibid., 1613.

minorities from the political process. If legislatures are free to enact facially neutral laws that suppress the practices of minority religions, then the Free Exercise Clause has, for all practical purposes, been stripped of its independent meaning. It has not been uncommon in the American experience for legislatures to be captured by fear and hostility to unfamiliar minority faiths. Jehovah's Witnesses, Mormons, even Catholics have experienced periods of persecution and hostility. Most cases relating to religious liberty under the Free Exercise Clause that have reached the United States Supreme Court have dealt with legislative enactments against minority religions. In the American system, the only branch of government that is required to listen to the complaints of religious minorities and render an unbiased decision is the judiciary. If that branch has now closed its doors in the wake of *Smith*, the inevitable consequence will be that many citizens sincerely holding religious beliefs that others might deem "unusual" will be forced to choose between abandoning their faith or being prosecuted for practicing it.

The *Smith* case is frightening in its implications for religious liberty. The Court's reason for the decision seems to be that religious liberty issues are difficult and their resolution is best left to the states. For the Court to simply relegate matters of religious liberty to the legislatures is an abdication of judicial responsibility of the worst kind. Moreover, to refuse to enforce rights that are expressly provided for in the Constitution is tantamount to the kind of judicial activism that justices like William Rehnquist have professed to be beyond the scope of the judiciary's constitutional mandate.

Many had assumed, prior to *Smith*, that the Supreme Court conservatives were "pro-religion." It was commonly believed, for example, that because William Rehnquist would allow nondiscriminatory government aid to religion under the Establishment Clause, he was, as chief justice, the "champion of religion" on the Court. As seen in the *Thomas* and *Smith* cases, however, this is not necessarily the case. Rehnquist's philosophy is one of accommodationism, but only to the extent that the various legislatures choose to exercise their prerogative to accommodate religion. Thus, the freedom of religion, and the protection against the establishment of religion, are not absolute; they are subordinated to the legislatures. Moreover, as seen in *Thomas* and in *Smith*, Rehnquist does not believe that the states' power to advance or interfere with religion should be over-restricted. It seems that he would vote to uphold virtually any law that does not directly and obviously interfere with religious exercise.[68] Based upon the *Smith* case, he now seems to have considerable like-minded company on the Court.

In summary, the Supreme Court, having moved to the right in its flight from strict separationism to "benevolent neutrality," now encounters the possibility of another move to the right in a flight from "benevolent neutrality" to accommodationism. Rehnquist's understanding of the religion clauses allows governments at all levels to accommodate and support religious practices if they choose to do so; likewise, governments at all levels may limit religious practices if they choose to do so. A government may "accommodate" a religious practice, or it may refuse to "accommodate" a religious practice, but the decision is left for the most part to the governmental authority. It is a federalism of the highest order, where states are accorded maximum freedom to tend to their own affairs. Such an approach, according to Rehnquist, would reduce the tension between the two religion clauses, reduce the unpredictability of results in the Supreme Court's current case-by-case handling of cases dealing with the religion clauses, and, most important, it would steer the Court toward alignment with the founding fathers' original intentions.

Chief Justice William Rehnquist has not staked out his accommodationist course lightly. The *Smith* case was a huge victory for the kind of accommodationist interpretation of the religion clauses advocated by Rehnquist. He seems now to have a number of justices following his lead to a narrower interpretation of the religion clauses. Future cases will bear close scrutiny on whether the Supreme Court will continue to move away from its traditional broad interpretations

---

68. Private school and Christian school advocates who see Rehnquist as the "champion of religion" on the Court would most certainly be disappointed to learn that Rehnquist has indicated that state and local administrative regulations imposed upon sectarian institutions dealing with, for example, curriculum, attendance, and certification, as well as requirements for fire and safety, are "properly placed." See *Jaffree*, 105 S. Ct. 2479 (1985), 2518. Such regulations are acceptable to Rehnquist because of his belief that legislatures should be free to run their own affairs.

of religion clauses to a Rehnquist-molded accommodationism. The final two chapters consider the propriety, prospects, and consequences of such a development in American church-state relations.

Chapter 8

AN EVALUATION OF THE REHNQUIST PERSPECTIVE IN THE LIGHT OF HISTORY

As a Supreme Court justice since 1971, and as chief justice since 1986, William Rehnquist has resolutely stood for the proposition that the original intentions of the constitutional framers is the binding norm for constitutional interpretation. The foregoing chapters have sought to articulate how Rehnquist's interpretations of the religion clauses of the First Amendment are guided by his understanding of the original intent of the framers. This chapter will offer an evaluation of that understanding in the light of certain historical realities.

Rehnquist expressed in *Jaffree* his determined belief that the framers of the religion clauses intended to accord religious liberty to all citizens (free exercise) and to prohibit the national government from establishing a church or favoring any denomination in preference to others (no establishment). These being the limits of the religion clauses, there is nothing, according to Rehnquist, in the religion clauses forbidding governments to accommodate religion in public spheres. For Rehnquist, in the contemporary setting, the essence of nonestablishment is the inability of one privileged church or any privileged combinations of churches to command government support. The federal government can, therefore, accommodate and support religion, provided there is no favoritism extended. Any government effort to control or favor designated churches would, in addition, run afoul of the free exercise guarantee.

If Rehnquist's understanding of the original meaning of the religion clauses is correct, then the Supreme Court has badly bungled its handling of church-state cases for the past half-century. The court has historically rejected accommodationism, believing instead that the religion clauses, and in particular the Establishment Clause, should be construed as giving the government no power whatsoever to aid or inhibit religion. Government is to be "neutral" with respect to religious matters, except that it should attempt to guard for everyone religious liberty and the free exercise of religion.

This "neutral" approach leaves the raising of money, the winning of adherents, the determination of doctrine, church government, ministry, and other religious matters to each religious body. Such a "separation" is not perfect or absolute. The Court has usually upheld, as examples, traditional practices of government chaplaincies, displays of religious symbols on public property, Sunday closing laws, the right of conscientious objection to war, and tax exemptions for religious organizations. All of these practices are technical violations of a strict doctrine of separation of church and state, but the Court has upheld them in its effort to avoid a hostility toward religion.

The Supreme Court has faced most of its difficulty—and criticism—in this separationist approach by rebuffing legislatures that seek to support various religious expressions, especially in the public schools, or to render financial support to churches or parochial schools. These twin pressures were recognized as early as 1947 by Justice Wiley Rutledge, who stated: "Two great drives are constantly in motion to abridge, in the name of education, the complete division of religion and civil authority which our forefathers made. One is to introduce religious education and observances into the public schools. The other, to obtain public funds for the aid and support of various private religious schools."[1] For the most part, the Supreme Court has adhered to a policy of separation in the face of constant challenges on these two, as well as other, fronts, although there have been occasional accommodationist exceptions.

---

1. *Everson v. Board of Education*, 330 U.S. 1 (1947), 63 (Rutledge, J., dissenting).

In setting its separationist policy, the Supreme Court has relied heavily upon the ideas concerning religious liberty advanced by such notables as Roger Williams, James Madison, and Thomas Jefferson. The Court has determined that, by and large, the views of such early American figures and the battles they fought in the advancement of their noble ideas, were instrumental, if not primary, in their effect on the final wording of the religion clauses. The Court has, therefore, looked behind the words of the First Amendment to discover the colonial drive for religious liberty, which had its purest expressions in the views of Williams, Jefferson, and Madison. The Court has historically considered the pronouncements of these giants in the battle for religious liberty to shed valuable light on the meaning of the rather tersely worded religion clauses.

Conversely, William Rehnquist, given to strict constructionism, focuses primarily on the words of the religion clauses, as elucidated by the proceedings of the First Congress and certain events thereafter. He is reluctant to go behind the words of the First Amendment to figures like Jefferson and Madison and their views on religious liberty. For Rehnquist, the battle for religious liberty in Virginia, in which Jefferson and Madison were leading figures, is not insignificant or unappreciated, only irrelevant to the proceedings of the First Congress. The goals and purposes of the First Congress with regard to religious liberty, says Rehnquist, were different from those of Jefferson and Madison in winning full religious liberty for Virginia in the years immediately before the commencement of the proceedings of the First Congress. For Rehnquist, while the views of Madison on religious liberty may have been revolutionary, they were, in full orb, implemented only in Virginia, not at the First Congress. What happened at the First Congress, according to Rehnquist, was more limited, and, moreover, occurred in relation to national, not state, concerns.

What should be made of these differences? Can the Jefferson-Madison separation imperative be seen in the words of the First Amendment? This chapter suggests an interpretation of the religion clauses that supports the Jefferson-Madison separation imperative. Accordingly, the following propositions are submitted as being crucial to an understanding of the background of the religion clauses: that the outstanding advocates for religious freedom in eighteenth-century America were Thomas Jefferson and James Madison; that they were strong advocates of the complete separation of church and state; and that their doctrine of separation of church and state was the continuation, and expansion, of a colonial revolution against many forms of establishment rather than an abrupt consummation of disestablishment.

The following additional propositions are submitted as being essential to an understanding of the meaning of the religion clauses as fashioned by the framers: that the religion clauses contain the budding expression of the doctrine of separation of church and state, the full expression of which was not to be realized until the second quarter of the nineteenth century, when the last of the states abolished their own religious establishments; that despite the infancy of the doctrine of the separation of church and state in 1789 at the First Congress, the founding fathers intended, in principle, to preclude any support of or interference with religion by the national government; and that early violations of the doctrine of separation of church and state were due to colonial practice and inheritance, and the inevitable overlapping concerns of church and state. Finally, it is submitted that the most important lesson that twentieth-century America can learn from the framers is that separationism guarantees religious liberty, while accommodationism threatens religious liberty.

These propositions are submitted as being indispensable to a full understanding of religious liberty as envisioned by the framers. They are propositions that run counter to William Rehnquist's own erudite interpretations of the religion clauses, which, it must be acknowledged, offer many valuable insights into the debate over the original intent of the framers. Moveover, it is not asserted here that the original intent of the framers can be determined with absolute certainty. The historical evidence does not permit absolutist conclusions. The framers and ratifiers of the Bill of Rights did not share a single understanding of the meaning, purpose, and implications of the religion clauses.

The framers lived in an age of transition in the development of relationships between church and state. The difficulty of breaking with traditional ideas on humankind, government, society, and religion resulted in an imbroglio so recondite that few could even enter the debate, much less give the right answers. To suggest that two hundred years later, we can unclutter the ambiguities and obscurities surrounding the original meaning of the religion clauses, and fashion the "right" church-state policy on the basis of that meaning, is intellectually dishonest. As Justice Byron White has written:

> One cannot seriously believe that the history of the First Amendment furnishes unequivocal answers to many of the fundamental issues of church-state relations. In the end, the courts have fashioned answers to these questions as best they can, the language of the Constitution and its history having left them a wide range of choice among many alternatives. But decision has been unavoidable; and, in choosing, the courts necessarily have carved out what they deemed to be the most desirable national policy governing various aspects of church-state relationships.[2]

Despite these limitations, it is prudent to search for the intent of the framers. The framers lived in a generation that was only beginning to understand that religion should be politically independent. That understanding is reflected, on a national level, in the Constitution and the First Amendment. In 1789, a similar understanding was being implemented in many, but not all of the states, which is why the First Amendment continued to leave religion in the hands of the states. Nevertheless, eventually, all of the states, on the model of the national government, took action to make religion independent of governmental influence.

The drive for religious liberty in early America was a revolution of incredible proportions, a revolution never successfully undertaken on soil outside of the United States. The religious liberty produced by this revolution was, in the words of Sanford H. Cobb, "the great gift of America to civilization and the world."[3] The framers sought to divorce religion from government. They did not seek to extinguish religion; for them, faith in the Almighty was the essence of life. However, to make religion dependent upon government was to depreciate true

---

2. *Committee for Public Education* v. *Nyquist*, 413 U.S. 756 (1973), 820.

3. Sanford H. Cobb, *The Rise of Religious Liberty in America: A History* (New York: Macmillan, 1902), 2.

religion; to rely upon government to throw its weight behind religion was to declare God impotent to further his purposes through voluntary means. Religion, a personal matter, was to remain politically independent and simultaneously furnish the moral basis for self-government.

The framers' purposes will shape one's understanding if they are taken seriously. Grasping their understanding of the role of religion in a democracy will enable one to avoid the trap of accommodationism—namely, that by seeking to give to religion a revered place by extending to it various aids and benefits, government unintentionally damages the authenticity of vital religion. That separationism was the intent of the framers can be seen in a review, albeit brief, of the influence on religious liberty of the Virginians, Jefferson and Madison.

The Virginia Struggle for Religious Liberty

The last quarter of the eighteenth century witnessed a historic revolution against the unholy alliance of church and state that had existed since Constantine's time. Roger Williams's early seventeenth-century concept of a "free church in a free society" at last triumphed in the United States.[4] One by one, the states began to sever ties between church and state. Before the nineteenth century, North Carolina (1776), New York (1777), Virginia (1786), South Carolina (1790), and Georgia (1798) all disestablished their churches, thereby offering them no further financial support.[5]

By far the most dramatic struggle for liberty and separation occurred in Virginia over a ten-year period, 1776-1786. There, religious minorities, especially Baptists, Methodists, and Presbyterians, aggressively fought for separation and they were vigorously supported by the less religiously orthodox Thomas Jefferson and James Madison.[6] Following

---

4. Wood, Thompson, and Miller, *Church and State*, 92.

5. Pennsylvania, Rhode Island, Delaware, and New Jersey never had established churches, leaving only Maryland, Connecticut, New Hampshire, and Massachusetts as nineteenth-century establishment holdovers among the original thirteen states. See Stokes, *Church and State*, 1:427-44.

6. Wood, Thompson, and Miller, *Church and State*, 92.

the outbreak of the American Revolution, the Church of England, established in Virginia since 1631,[7] was for all practical purposes disestablished in Virginia by a statute in late 1776 that exempted all nonmembers from taxes for its support. Thus the Church of England received no government support after 1776. The statute of 1776 left open, however, the question of whether religion ought to be placed on a private, voluntary basis or be supported on a nonpreferential basis by a new "general" assessment.[8]

In 1779, a bill for support on a nonpreferential basis was introduced; in response, Jefferson introduced his "Bill for Establishing Religious Freedom," providing, in part, "that no man shall be compelled to frequent or support any religious worship, place, or ministry whatsoever." The bill also strikingly declared that "Almighty God hath created the mind free" and that all attempts to control it by the imposition of civil disabilities were "a departure from the plan of the Holy Author of our religion, who being Lord of both body and mind, yet chose not to propagate it by coercions on either." It was "sinful and tyrannical" to compel a man to contribute to the propagation "of opinions which he disbelieves or abhors." Truth would prevail if left alone; it had nothing to fear "from the conflict of error."[9]

Jefferson's motivation for introducing the bill was his belief that religion was a personal matter and that government should exercise no jurisdiction over religion, including the granting of financial support to any church. By contrast, the assessment bill was predicated on the supposition, expressed in its preamble, that the state must encourage religion. The bill sought to make Christianity "the established religion," whereby each taxpayer would have the right to designate the church of his preference, and that church alone would receive his taxes; money collected from a taxpayer failing to designate a church was to be divided proportionately among all churches of his county.[10]

Faced with two diametrically opposed bills, the Virginia legislature engaged in prolonged debate, lasting weeks, only to deadlock; neither

---

7. Ibid., 83.
8. Levy, "The Original Meaning," 75.
9. Virginia Statute for Establishing Religious Freedom; see Appendix A.
10. Levy, "The Original Meaning," 75.

bill passed. Frustrated with the failure of the legislature to support Christianity, Patrick Henry introduced in 1784 another general assessment bill to require "a moderate tax or contribution annually for the support of the Christian religion, or of some Christian church, denomination or communion of Christians, or for some form of Christian worship."[11] Madison opposed the bill but a majority favored establishment, and he averted certain passage only by winning postponement of a final vote on the bill until the following term.

Madison, assuming primary leadership in the struggle for full religious liberty during Jefferson's service in France, brought his case to the people by writing and circulating his celebrated "Memorial and Remonstrance Against Religious Assessments." In the "Remonstrance," Madison made the point that the issue was not whether religion was necessary, but whether an establishment was necessary for religion. Man was naturally religious, he maintained, but history suggested that establishments corrupted the religious impulse. The assessment bill, he maintained, would dishonor Christianity because it, along with all religion, was not within the purview of civil authority.[12] Throughout the "Remonstrance," Madison referred to the proposed assessment as an "establishment." This is significant because the bill that Madison fought so arduously against called for the support of all Christian denominations, clearly an act on the order of nonpreferential support of religion. To suggest, then, as Rehnquist and other accommodationists do, that Madison was in favor of nonpreferential support of religion in the later debates on the First Amendment makes Madison out to be remarkably inconsistent.

Madison's efforts against the assessment bill proved successful. A newly elected legislature allowed the bill to die unnoticed. Madison then reintroduced Jefferson's "Bill for Religious Freedom," which prohibited altogether government support of religion. Jefferson's bill

---

11. Quoted in ibid., 76.

12. For a detailed study of Madison's legislative efforts for religious liberty in Virginia, including a summary of speeches he made in session in opposition to Henry's assessment bill, see Lance Banning, "James Madison, the Statute for Religious Freedom, and the Crisis of Republican Convictions," in The Virginia Statute for Religious Freedom, ed. Merrill D. Peterson and Robert C. Vaughan (Cambridge: Cambridge University Press, 1988): 109-38.

passed by an overwhelming vote of sixty-seven to twenty in January 1786.[13]

The struggle for religious liberty in Virginia was described by Jefferson as the most difficult of his career;[14] Madison's efforts were equally indefatigable. Jefferson's "Statute" and Madison's "Remonstrance" were twin instruments that marked a major turning point in the development of the doctrine of separation of church and state in the United States. During the Constitutional Convention the following year, Jefferson was still in France, but of Madison, it has been said that the "lessons that he learned from the Virginia struggle over church and state were probably the most important catalyst for the conclusions that became his most distinctive contribution to the Founding."[15]

It is difficult to conceive how the First Amendment prohibited only the designation of one church as a national one, or the preference of certain denominations over others, when seven states, including Virginia, had altogether abandoned governmental support of religion by 1789.[16] In all of those states, government support of *any* church or churches was considered contrary to the basic principles of religious liberty. Moreover, the remaining six of the original thirteen states followed suit after 1789 and abolished the right of their legislatures to support or "establish" religion.[17] These steps by the states indicate a prevailing mood of separation, which meant, primarily, the proscription of support of religion by civil authority. It was a revolution "in process" in 1789, the fullest expression of which was in Virginia, the final results of which were only to be realized in years to come in the other states.

Leonard Levy makes an additional point of considerable weight.

13. Levy, "The Original Meaning," 76.
14. Banning, "James Madison," 113.
15. Ibid., 109.
16. The other six states, in addition to Virginia, were Delaware, New Jersey, Rhode Island, and Pennsylvania, none of which ever had establishments, and New York and North Carolina.
17. The disestablishments occurred in the following order: South Carolina (1790), Georgia (1798), Maryland (1810), Connecticut (1818), New Hampshire (1819), and Massachusetts (1833).

Accommodationists typically hold that the prohibition against "establishment" in the First Amendment was intended to ban the preference for one church, denomination, or sect over others, in the sense of the European tradition of nations having only *one* established church. However, says Levy, a close examination of the historical record reveals that after 1776 no state in America had a mode of establishment that restricted itself to a system of support of one church or sect alone. There were six states that maintained establishments after 1776 (Massachusetts, New Hampshire, Connecticut, Maryland, Georgia, South Carolina), but in each of these states, the establishments were not single, but multiple. That is, all of the six states that continued to provide public support for religion extended their establishments to several different religious groups, not just one.

From this observation, it can be convincingly argued, as Levy has done, that "an establishment of religion in America at the time of the framing of the Bill of Rights meant government aid and sponsorship of religion, principally by impartial tax support of the institutions of religion, the churches."[18] Levy concludes, then, that when the First Amendment was drafted in 1789, the framers understood that they were prohibiting governmental support of religion in general, and support of all churches, not just one or several. No member of the First Congress came from a state that supported an exclusive establishment of religion; no such example, says Levy, could be found among the states.[19]

When viewed from the perspective of the progressive development of religious liberty, Thomas Jefferson's letter to the Danbury Baptist Association in 1802, stating that the purpose of the First Amendment was to create "a wall of separation between church and state," is raised to its rightful place as a meaningful expression of the intentions of the framers. Indeed, it was this "wall of separation" metaphor that Justice Hugo Black appropriately resorted to in announcing the Court's broad interpretation of the Establishment Clause in the *Everson* case in 1947. In adopting the "wall of separation" metaphor, the Court

---

18. Levy, "The Original Meaning," 77.
19. Ibid.

was giving full credence to the monumental efforts for religious liberty of not only Thomas Jefferson, but Jefferson's separationist equal and fellow Virginian, James Madison.

Early Violations of the Separation Doctrine

In Chapter 6, in the presentation of Rehnquist's understanding of the formation of the religion clauses, it was shown that Rehnquist looks to a number of early mixtures of government and religion to support his view that the framers never intended to impose any type of institutional separation between the national government and religion. It may be helpful now, in the present evaluation of Rehnquist's perspective on the religion clauses, to come back to those practices cited by Rehnquist—presidential proclamations of days of prayer and thanksgiving, and the issue of the advocacy of religion in the Northwest Ordinance—and offer some explanation of how these practices could have occurred without necessarily being inconsistent with the separationist approach to the religion clauses.

As noted earlier, the practices of presidential proclamations of days of prayer and thanksgiving began with George Washington and have been sanctioned by many presidents throughout this nation's history. These are practices that, indeed, violate the notion of a strict separation of church and state, but their constitutionality has usually been taken for granted in keeping with a "common sense" interpretation of the First Amendment.[20]

Government proclamations of thanksgiving and prayer began during the period of the Continental Congress, which legislated on such matters as sin, repentance, humiliation, mourning, public worship, funerals, doctrine, chaplains, and other religious matters. Resolutions fixing days for thanksgiving, prayer, and fasting were commonplace. Upon the establishment of the new Constitution, with its concept of religion being beyond the purview of the federal government, most of these practices disappeared. A few continued, however. Congres-

---

20. Pfeffer, *Church, State, and Freedom*, 223.

sional chaplaincy was one; government proclamation of Thanksgiving Day was another. These practices, which have continued off and on since the First Congress, are best explained as holdovers from the colonial period and as practices deemed substantially harmless by most governmental leaders who sought to acknowledge God's authority over all things in heaven and earth.[21]

It would be erroneous, however, to assume that the constitutionality of these practices has always been accepted without question. When, in the First Congress after the adoption of the Constitution, a resolution was offered to request the president to "recommend to the People of the United States a day of Thanksgiving and Prayer, to be observed by acknowledging with grateful hearts the many signal favours of Almighty God,"[22] objection was raised by a number of the members of Congress. Thomas Tucker of South Carolina, for example, suggested that "it is a business with which the Congress have nothing to do; it is a religious matter, and as such is proscribed to us."[23] Despite this objection, the resolution passed, and in 1789 Washington proclaimed a national day of thanksgiving, which he followed with several others during his administration.

While Washington made every effort to frame his proclamations in language acceptable to all faiths, his successor, John Adams, called for Christian worship. Jefferson refused to issue any religious proclamations, believing that "the Constitution has precluded them."[24] Madison objected to the practice in principle, but was unable to resist the demands and used prayers with "general terms, for which he was criticized" by those who thought he should have inserted "particulars according with the faith of certain Christian sects."[25]

With one exception, Madison's successors followed his example, and issued prayer and thanksgiving proclamations in nonsectarian language. The one exception was Andrew Jackson, who shared Jefferson's views and steadfastly refused to issue any thanksgiving procla-

---

21. Ibid.
22. Stokes, *Church and State*, 1:486.
23. Ibid., 1:486-87.
24. Quoted in Pfeffer, *Church, State, and Freedom*, 224.
25. Ibid.

mations because he thought he "might disturb the security which religion now enjoys in the country, in its complete separation from the political concerns of the General Government."[26]

In sum, presidential proclamations of prayer and thanksgiving should be viewed as exceptions to the basic constitutional requirement of separation. They certainly are not as harmful as other types of government encroachments on religious affairs, although many current national legislators, who absent themselves from the daily opening prayer of the congressional chaplains, would beg to disagree.[27]

In his *Jaffree* dissent, Rehnquist also invoked the Northwest Ordinance as an indicator that the First Congress did not wish to divorce totally religion from government. As previously noted, the Northwest Ordinance of 1787 recited that "religion, morality, and knowledge, being necessary to good government and the happiness of mankind, schools and the means of education shall forever be encouraged."[28] This ordinance can also be viewed as a carryover from the practice of the Continental Congress to legislate regarding religious matters; the legislation was actually passed before consideration of the religion clauses was undertaken by the First Congress in 1789.

In addition, education in the eighteenth century was almost universally regarded as a matter for church concern and control, and, therefore, outside the jurisdiction of the federal government. The concept of widespread public education was only in its genesis in 1787. The Northwest Ordinance, however, called for "the maintenance of public schools." In all likelihood, it was assumed that the churches would continue to play a significant role in the supervision of education in the territories.[29] The apparent inconsistency, then, with a doctrine of separation of church and state, on the one hand, and governmental encouragement of religion in territorial public schools, on the other hand, is therefore reconciled. Once again, the notion that the United States was in a time of transition—moving away from church-state

---

26. Ibid.

27. John M. Swomley, *Religious Liberty and the Secular State* (Buffalo, N.Y.: Prometheus Books, 1987), 54.

28. *United States Code* 1:x1iii (1976 Edition).

29. Pfeffer, *Church, State, and Freedom*, 478-79.

union to church-state separation—accounts for most of the early governmental religious practices, including the mix of religion and civil authority appearing in the Northwest Ordinance.

Accommodationism and Separationism Contrasted

To its credit, accommodationism seeks to give to religion an honored role in American society. It is, arguably, a reaction to the perceived declining role of religion in America. Granted, the United States has witnessed a social upheaval of dramatic proportions in the last half of the twentieth century. Crime, alcoholism, teenage pregnancy, drugs, suicide, racial tension, and a host of other problems have reached crisis levels. Simultaneously, interest in religion has supposedly declined. A Gallup poll reported that in 1957 only 14 percent of Americans believed that religion was losing its influence. In 1967, however, 57 percent held this opinion, and in 1970 those who believed religion was losing influence increased to 75 percent.[30]

For many, the country's social problems could be traced, at least in part, to some of the decisions of the Supreme Court, especially those striking down religious exercises in the public schools. For example, there was an uproar of public dissent after the Court's holding in *Engel* v. *Vitale* (1962),[31] which banned officially prescribed prayers in the nation's public schools. According to one source, one U.S. Congressman charged, "Only a court composed of agnostics could find anything wrong with this prayer. The Court has now officially stated its disbelief in God Almighty."[32] Billy Graham condemned the ruling as "another step toward the secularization of the United States."[33] An editorial in *America*, a weekly Jesuit publication, suggested that 25 June 1962 (the day the decision was announced) deserved to be called "Black

---

30. Robert T. Handy, *A Christian America: Protestant Hopes and Historical Realities*, 2nd ed. (New York: Oxford University Press, 1984), 191.

31. 370 U.S. 421 (1962).

32. James E. Wood, Jr., "Religion Sponsored by the State," *Journal of Church and State* 4 (November 1962): 141. The author did not identify the quoted Congressman.

33. "Uproar Over School Prayer—And the Aftermath," *U.S. News and World Report* 53, 9 July 1962, 44.

Monday," in recognition of the author of the Court's majority opinion, Hugo Black. Its assessment of the Court's decision was poignant: "It is not only an unpopular decision with the vast majority of the American people. It is quite literally, a stupid decision, a doctrinaire decision, an unrealistic decision, a decision that spits in the face of our history, our tradition and our heritage as a religious people."[34]

Similar acrimony was directed to the Court after other cases, notably the *Stone* v. *Graham*[35] decision in 1980, which denied the right of Kentucky public schools to post a copy of the Ten Commandments in their classrooms, and the 1985 decision in *Wallace* v. *Jaffree*,[36] in which the Court struck down Alabama's "moment of silence" legislation as an advancement of religion. Following the *Jaffree* case, Attorney General Edwin Meese accused the Court of undermining religion.[37] Likewise, Secretary of Education William Bennett suggested that the Court had a "disdain for education as well as religion."[38]

Yet to blame society's dramatic alteration in mores on the Supreme Court is fatuous as well as insupportable. No sociological explanation seems adequate to explain the social trauma seen in America in recent decades. Surely it has had more to do with the searing of society caused by the student revolts of the late 1960s and the "revolution of rights" of the sixties and seventies than it has had to do with various decisions handed down by the Supreme Court.

Whatever the cause of society's current problems, few would argue that America is more secularized today than at any time in its history. The notion that America is becoming increasingly so is a stated belief of William Rehnquist. In *Meek* v. *Pittinger*,[39] Rehnquist accused the Court majority of throwing "its weight on the side of those who believe that our society as a whole should be a secular one."[40] The theory adhered to by Rehnquist, it seems, is that the Supreme Court, in the interest of protecting the sensitivities of those who are likely

---

34. "Black Monday Decision," *America* 107 (7 July 1962): 456.
35. 449 U.S. 39 (1980).
36. 105 S. Ct. 2479 (1985).
37. Meese Speech, 464.
38. Ibid., 462.
39. 421 U.S. 349 (1975).
40. Ibid., 395 (Rehnquist, J., dissenting).

to be offended by religious expressions, has bent too far and become more favorable to irreligion than to religion. This was not the intent of the framers, Rehnquist contends. The solution for Rehnquist and other accommodationists is, apparently, a nurturing of religion by government.

Unfortunately, accommodationism is mistaken in its belief that religion should be nurtured, patronized, or promoted by government. The issue is really whether religion needs the state to "prop it up," or whether religion thrives best when left alone. Accommodationism prefers government sponsorship and subsidy of religion rather than allowing it to compete on its merits against indifference and irreligion. The Jeffersonian and Madisonian views, that religion will exist in far greater purity without the support of government, is rejected. Both Jefferson and Madison recognized that only voluntary religion is authentic and that government nurture desecrates true religion.

If all churches and religious organizations were to be entitled to nonpreferential aid from government, which is the accommodationist position, one can only imagine the energy and dollars that would be spent in the competition for government support. Inevitably, those with the most political influence and financial resources would benefit the most, the result being the denial of the rights of religious minorities. The better solution is to prohibit government support of religion. In the words of a prominent American Catholic theologian, John Courtney Murray, religion should not be state-supported "for the essentially theological reason that religion is of its nature a personal, private interior matter of the individual conscience, having no relevance to the public concerns of the state."[41]

Cases like *Engel*, *Stone*, and *Jaffree*, for which the Supreme Court is often excoriated, even by Rehnquist, are determined efforts by the Court to honor the great principles of religious liberty so profoundly expressed by Jefferson and Madison. The unfortunate misconception in the current debate over church-state relations in the United States is that the doctrine of separation of church and state is anti-religious.

---

41. John Courtney Murray, "Law and Prepossessions," *Law and Contemporary Problems* 14 (Winter 1949): 29.

To the contrary, it is the great protector of true religion, and leaves the individual alone to decide upon and live out his religious beliefs. David Little insightfully traces the convictions of Jefferson and Madison on this point through Roger Williams:

> He [Williams] simply believed (as did Jefferson and Madison) that the connections [between religion and a secular civil order] had to be worked out by each individual, alone or in groups, on the basis of independent conscientious consideration. For Williams, that could happen only in a society in which the civil order knew, and knew profoundly, its secular limitations—knew, that is, that religious belief and values are, from a civil point of view, never settled, never closed, but are forever open to what Williams described as continual "chewing and weighing." Too much emphasis on an easy compatibility between religion and the civil order would . . . corrupt religion and debase the civil order, as Williams believed had happened over and over again in the bloody experience of post-Constantinian Christianity. The same vision as well as the same fears found their way into Jefferson's Statute and Madison's "Memorial and Remonstrance."[42]

A related criticism of the principle of separation of church and state is that it mandates a secular state. The idea of a secular state, however, is not hostile to religion. A secular state, on the model of the United States, is uncommitted to any religious institution or any religious beliefs. Religion is left to the people who are free to choose their own beliefs about God, the universe, worship, human nature, and other religious matters. A secular state, then, guarantees religious liberty, including the right to propagate one's own religious beliefs.[43]

Philip Schaff, the distinguished nineteenth-century church historian, wrote that the U.S. Constitution "is neither hostile nor friendly to any religion; it is simply silent on the subject, as lying beyond the jurisdiction of the general government."[44] If the state attempts

---

42. David Little, "Religion and Civil Virtue in America: Jefferson's Statute Reconsidered," in *The Virginia Statute for Religious Freedom*, ed. Merrill D. Peterson and Robert C. Vaughan (Cambridge: Cambridge University Press, 1988), 250.

43. Swomley, *Religious Liberty*, 7, 14.

44. James E. Wood, Jr., "The Secular State," *Journal of Church and State* 7 (Spring 1965): 175, quoting Philip Schaff.

to support all religions, it compels those who claim no religion at all—their right in a secular state—to support what they do not believe. Even if all taxes collected for religious purposes were dispensed to the church of a taxpayer's choice, it may be in a different amount than that which he or she would voluntarily have given. Any such arrangement is not religious liberty. Madison was emphatic on this point in the "Remonstrance"—that to require a person to support even the religion of his own choice denied him his freedom of choice and his right to religious liberty.

John Swomley has summarized several reasons why churches should favor separation of church and state. Among his reasons are these five primary ones:

(1) Separation prevents the government from determining church policy, whether directly or indirectly.

(2) Separation does not permit churches to seek special privileges from government that are denied to minority religious groups and to nonreligious citizens.

(3) Churches are healthier and stronger if they assume responsibility both for financing their own programs and for stimulating their members to accept that responsibility.

(4) By operating independently of government aid, the churches deny to government the imposition of compulsory tithes on all taxpayers, believers and nonbelievers alike.

(5) Since separation precludes financial support or special privilege from government, the churches are free to engage in prophetic criticism of the government and to work for social justice.[45]

Separationism is not a threat to religious life in the United States. Despite what appears to be an increasing secularization, church membership in America is at an all time high. Under a commitment to the separation of church and state, church membership has reportedly climbed from 12 percent in 1800 to 35 percent in 1900, to 50 percent in 1950, to 62 percent in 1963, and to 80 percent in 1987.[46] Ac-

45. Swomley, Religious Liberty, 14-15.

46. James E. Wood, Jr., "Religion and the Public Schools," Brigham Young University Law Review 86 (Fall 1986): 353; Henry J. Abraham, "Religion, the Constitution, the Court, and Society: Some Contemporary Reflections on Mandates,

commodationism, it could be argued, offers a much greater threat to American religious life than separationism. The threat of accommodation, however, does not lie in its intention to damage religion; its threat lies, ironically, in its intention to elevate religion. When government involves itself in religious matters, religion is profaned and, sadly, religious liberty is destroyed.

Accommodationism as Embracing Both Establishment and Free Exercise

It should be clear by now that accommodationism, as a way of understanding the religion clauses, permits governmental support of religion, so long as it is done in a nondiscriminatory way. For William Rehnquist, this fundamental aspect of accommodationism springs from a narrow interpretation of the Establishment Clause. Yet, as already seen, Rehnquist's narrow interpretation of the Free Exercise Clause seems to restrict individual religious liberty. How does a position of accommodation of religion square with a position of restricted free exercise of religion? Are Rehnquist's positions contradictory? The answer is yes if one incorrectly understands Rehnquist only as a strong advocate of religion. The answer is no, however, if one correctly understands Rehnquist, fundamentally, as a strong advocate of majoritarian-based democracy.

Rehnquist does not see his role on the Supreme Court to be one of opening the doors to religion in America's public schools and other public sectors. That might happen under his judicial application of the Establishment Clause, but it will happen only if state and local governments, acting under the mandates of their electorates, permit it to happen. The Establishment Clause permits that kind of accommodation of religion, Rehnquist would say, so long as the advancement of religion is nondiscriminatory, that is, that no sects or faiths are

---

Words, Human Beings, and the Art of the Possible," in *How Does the Constitution Protect Religious Freedom?* (Washington, D.C.: American Enterprise Institute, 1987): 16; Miller and Flowers, *Toward Benevolent Neutrality*, 2.

legislatively excluded from fair treatment. However, for Rehnquist, the natural corollary to the permissible accommodation of religion under the Establishment Clause is the permissible restriction on the free exercise of religion. As indicated in his lengthy dissent in *Thomas*, and by his vote in *Smith*, if state and local governments pass valid, generally applicable laws prohibiting conduct that unfortunately conflict with a citizen's religious beliefs or conduct, then the governmental regulation will prevail. As Justice Scalia wrote in the *Smith* case, this is the "unavoidable consequence of democratic government."[47] This restrictive approach to free exercise jurisprudence, which acts as a potential burden on the religious liberty of minorities that even Scalia admits to, operates consistently with "accommodationism." On the one hand, the accommodationist interpretation of the Establishment Clause leads to the accommodation of religion. On the other hand, however, the accommodationist interpretation of the Free Exercise Clause accommodates not religion, necessarily, but a principle—deference to majoritarian democracy at the state and local level.

It is therefore to be acknowledged, to the credit of Chief Justice Rehnquist, that he offers a remarkably harmonious approach to interpreting and applying two religion clauses that on their face might seem to contradict one another. His narrow interpretations of the religion clauses certainly reduce the ubiquitous and problematic "tension" between the clauses, clearly one of the goals he has set for the Supreme Court in its handling of church-state issues. Certain questions must be asked however. Is the reduction of the tension between the religion clauses a valid objective? Does not the broad wording of the religion clauses demand broad interpretations? Moreover, can the religion clauses be understood as unitary, not contradictory, in their purposes, and yet still be broadly interpreted?

The broad interpretations given to the religion clauses by the Supreme Court since *Cantwell* in 1940 have been on the basis of its understanding of the original intent of the founding fathers. The Court justices have acknowledged that there is an inherent tension in the clauses and have often voiced some measure of frustration over

---

47. 110 S. Ct. 1595, 1606.

the task of properly interpreting two clauses with different functions, each of which was cast by the founding fathers as a sweeping, absolute prohibition.[48]

The language of the religion clauses is general, not specific. Chief Justice Warren Burger acknowledged this point in *Walz* in commenting that the purpose of the framers was to "state an objective, not to write a statute."[49] A starting point in modern interpretation of the religion clauses should be the assumption that the framers intentionally worded the religion clauses in language that was broad and general. If they had wanted to write a detailed list of specific rules regarding religion with an equally detailed list of exceptions, they could have done so. Attempts at greater specificity were rejected at the First Congress (see Chapter 4). Do the broad principles stated in the text have implications that the framers did not foresee? Of course. But it is also reasonable to assume that the framers thought about this point, and therefore agreed on broad language that would permit flexibility in later applications.

That there was some degree of tension between the religion clauses was undoubtedly recognized by the framers. Madison, for one, understood the difficulty of harmonizing the clauses in all situations: "It may not be easy, in every possible case, to trace the line of separation between the rights of religions and the Civil authority with such distinctness as to avoid collisions. . . ."[50] The Supreme Court frequently has acknowledged this tension between the clauses, recognizing their broad language in which each clause is cast in absolute terms. William Rehnquist's narrow reading of both religion clauses, however, does not do justice to the clauses' purposefully broad language. His reading of them is rigid enough to defeat their basic purpose, which was to ensure that no religion be "sponsored or favored, none commanded, and none inhibited."[51] More specifically, his nonpreferential reading of the Establishment Clause should be rejected, because such a reading,

---

48. See, for example, *Walz* v. *Tax Commission*, 397 U.S. 664 (1970), 668.
49. Ibid.
50. Letter to Rev. Adams (1832), Gaillard Hunt, ed., *The Writings of James Madison* (New York: n.p., 1904), 9:487.
51. *Walz* v. *Tax Commission*, 397 U.S. 664 (1970), 669.

as already seen, was clearly rejected in the proceedings of the First Congress. His narrow reading of the Free Exercise Clause should likewise be rejected, because it denies what the framers expressly sought to provide for in passing the Bill of Rights, namely, the protection of the fundamental civil liberties of minorities from majoritarian-based government. Both readings represent an accommodationism not likely contemplated by the founding fathers.

Even if Rehnquist is correct in characterizing the religion clauses as having more unity than tension in their intended interrelationship, the result need not be the narrow interpretations of the clauses that he argues for, but the broad interpretations that the Supreme Court historically has decided upon. Leo Pfeffer, an eminent church-state scholar who is also an ardent separationist, takes the position that the religion clauses were originally intended to encompass a unitary guaranty of separation and freedom. He has written: "Separation and freedom are not separate concepts or principles but really two sides of a single coin. The Fathers of the First Amendment were convinced that the free exercise of religion and the separation of church and state were two ways of saying the same thing: that separation guaranteed freedom and freedom required separation."[52]

Pfeffer is not the only scholar to hold this view. Professor Philip Kurland of the University of Chicago has summarized his position as follows: "The freedom and separation clauses should be read as stating a single precept: that government cannot utilize religion as a standard for action or inaction because these clauses, read together as they should be, prohibit classification in terms of religion either to confer a benefit or to impose a burden."[53] Similar pronouncements have come from members of the Supreme Court. For example, Justice Wiley Rutledge, in a dissenting opinion in the *Everson* case, said:

---

52. Leo Pfeffer, "Freedom and/or Separation: The Constitutional Dilemma of the First Amendment," *Minnesota Law Review* 64 (1980): 561. For an excellent article by Pfeffer arguing for a unitary view of the religion clauses, see Leo Pfeffer, "The Unity of the First Amendment Religion Clauses," in *The First Freedom: Religion and the Bill of Rights*, ed. James E. Wood, Jr. (Waco, Tex.: Dawson Institute of Church-State Studies, 1990): 133-66.

53. Philip Kurland, *Religion and the Law: Of Church and State and the Supreme Court* (Chicago: Aldine Publishing Co., 1962), 112.

" 'Establishment' and 'free exercise' were correlative and coextensive ideas, representing only different facts of the single great and fundamental freedom."[54] Justice Rutledge's view was the dominant view of the members of the Supreme Court, who, prior to the 1970s, regularly gave broad, separationist readings to the religion clauses. It was only during the decades of the 1970s and 1980s that various members of the Court began to frequently refer to conflicts between the establishment and free exercise clauses.

The point of alluding to the unitary view of the religion clauses held by Leo Pfeffer, Philip Kurland, Justice Wiley Rutledge, and, in general, most of the individual justices of the Supreme Court before 1970 or so, is to show that the religion clauses can be broadly construed (separation of church and state; generous grants of free exercise) in a conceptual framework that sees little tension between the separate clauses. In this way, then, Chief Justice Rehnquist's argument for a more unitary approach to interpreting and applying the religion clauses does not necessarily hold up. Instead, it can readily be shown that even among many of those who, like Rehnquist, see little tension between the clauses, the preferred readings of the religion clauses are broad, not narrow.

The Supreme Court is, ultimately, the final arbiter on the kinds of encroachments that will be permitted on religious liberty. Due to accommodationist interpretations of the religion clauses of the First Amendment by various members of the Court, among them Chief Justice Rehnquist, there does exist the very real possibility that the Supreme Court could become an accommodationist Court in this century. The possibility of such an unprecedented development and its potential effect on American church-state relations is the subject of this book's next and final chapter.

---

54. *Everson v. Board of Education*, 330 U.S. 1 (1947), 40.

Chapter 9

REHNQUIST, THE RELIGION CLAUSES, AND FUTURE DIRECTIONS OF THE SUPREME COURT

Separationism, Neutrality, and Accommodation: Where Is the Court Headed?

Until the *Smith* case, few Supreme Court observers were worried that the Free Exercise Clause was in jeopardy. Before the *Smith* ruling on 17 April 1990, the Court had held that a government must show a "compelling state interest" before restricting religious freedom and must prove that no less intrusive means is available to achieve its goal. This standard had generally been applicable since the 1963 case of *Sherbert* v. *Verner*.

The *Smith* result surprised everyone—liberals and conservatives alike—and it was difficult to find anyone—liberals or conservatives— happy about the decision's potential impact on religious liberty. Representative Stephen Solarz from New York remarked, "With a stroke of a pen, the Supreme Court virtually removed religious freedom—our first freedom—from the Bill of Rights."[1] Robert L. Maddox of Americans United for Separation of Church and State expressed similar sentiments: "The right to free exercise of religion is a basic constitutional principle guaranteed in our Bill of Rights. The Supreme

---

1. Quoted in *Church and State* 48 (September 1990): 13.

Court's recent *Smith* decision demoted that essential right to the status of a constitutional afterthought."[2]

However, it may still be too early to make rash predictions about *Smith's* permanence. Given the considerable amount of verbal acrimony from every corner directed the Court's way since the *Smith* decision, not to mention the scholarly ink that has flowed in its critique, there remains the possibility that the *Smith* case could eventually be reversed or significantly modified. Moreover, legislation from Congress is expected to attempt to restore the "compelling state interest" test. It is probable that the legislation will be supported by the Bush administration. Of course, there is no guarantee that such legislation, or similar acts passed by the states, will pass tests of constitutionality if the United States Supreme Court one day is asked to review such remedial laws. So, the *Smith* case and its potential impact on religious liberty remains fraught with uncertainties.

The *Smith* decision was a monumental victory for Chief Justice Rehnquist and those who share his approach to interpreting the religion clauses. While the result upholds federalism, it seriously erodes the notion of religious liberty as an inviolable, unalienable freedom standing beyond the reach of the law. The *Smith* case is a completed step one in a two-step process that would make the Rehnquist Court an accommodationist Court. The second step would be a complete abandonment of the *Lemon* three-part test, the cornerstone of the Court's separationist interpretations of the Establishment Clause, and the replacement of it with an accommodationist interpretation of the Establishment Clause. The remainder of this chapter focuses on that eventuality and some of the possible effects.

While there are seminal links between the Establishment Clause and the Free Exercise Clause, the latter has spawned far less litigation than the former. Moreover, the separationist-accommodationist controversy springs primarily, though not exclusively, from varying interpretations of the Establishment Clause. The search for the meaning of the phrase "Congress shall make no law respecting an establishment of religion" inexorably marches on without agreement on what the

---

2. Ibid.

ennobled framers meant by those hallowed ten words.

This is somewhat surprising, it is submitted, because to Jefferson and Madison, and their many devoted followers, the principle of separation was absolutely indispensable to the basic freedoms of belief, conscience, and dissent. Hostility to religion was not in their hearts— they simply regarded religion as an entirely *private* matter. Their guiding conviction was that the state as secular authority has jurisdiction only over *temporal* matters, not *spiritual* matters.

In reflecting upon the current status of the relationship between church and state in the United States, one wonders what must have happened to alter the spirit and intent of the noble principles of Jefferson and Madison and their large following. There certainly exists no uniform commitment to such principles on the current Supreme Court. The retreat from a solid commitment to separationism has led to considerable confusion about the Court's approach to Establishment Clause adjudication. For example, Senator Daniel Patrick Moynihan (Democrat, New York), in reflecting upon the rather unpredictable nature of Establishment Clause cases, remarked in 1979 that "in the years since 1947 [the *Everson* case] . . . the Court's decisions have become ever more confused and contradictory," resulting in "an intellectual shambles: one confused and convoluted decision, requiring a yet more confused and convoluted explanation or modification."[3] Antonin Scalia, then a U.S. Court of Appeals judge (appointed to the Supreme Court in 1986), had similar sentiments: "[The] Supreme Court jurisprudence concerning the Establishment Clause in general, and the application of that clause to governmental assistance for religiously affiliated education in particular, is in a state of utter chaos and unpredictable change."[4]

In light of the dizzy state of Supreme Court Establishment Clause holdings, it is surely fair to ask the question of where the Court now stands on the separation-accommodation scale, and where it is headed. Officially, the Supreme Court's yardstick for testing the absence of an Establishment Clause violation is the *Lemon* three-part test. That

---

3. "What Do You Do When the Supreme Court Is Wrong?" *Public Interest* 57 (Fall 1979): no page given; quoted by Abraham, "Religion and the Constitution," 24.

4. As reported by Ruth Marcus, *Washington Post*, 23 June 1986, 17, quoted by Abraham, "Religion and the Constitution," 24.

test is, by way of review, that the legislation in question is not deemed an establishment of religion if it (1) has a secular purpose, (2) neither advances nor inhibits religion, and (3) does not cause an excessive entanglement between religion and government. The *Lemon* test represents the Court's effort to be neutral in religious matters—neither hostile nor capitulating toward religion, just neutral. The philosophy of neutrality was first used in *Abington School District* v. *Schempp*,[5] in which the Court disallowed official public school practices of Bible reading and reciting of the Lord's Prayer. Justice Tom Clark, a devout Presbyterian, wrote for the Court:

> The place of religion in our society is an exalted one, achieved through a long reliance on the home, the church and the inviolable citadel of the individual heart and mind. We have come to recognize through bitter experience that it is not within the power of government to invade that citadel, whether its purpose or effect be to aid or oppose, to advance or retard. *In the relationship between man and religion, the state is firmly committed to a position of neutrality.*[6]

Unofficially, many members of the Court stray from the Court's declared "neutral" philosophy. Those who are "hard-line" on the *Lemon* test tend toward being strong separationists. Those who are "soft" on the *Lemon* test tend toward being accommodationists. A third category of justices should also be mentioned—those who are neither "hard-line" nor "soft," but somewhat pliable, flexible, and sometimes unpredictable as "swing-votes"; these members might be called centrists and are, in general, actually closest to the Court's official position of "neutrality."

These three modes of Establishment Clause interpretation can be illustrated by a brief look at how the justices lined up in the 1987 case of *Edwards* v. *Aguillard*,[7] the celebrated "scientific-creationism" case. Louisiana's "Creationism Act" forbade the teaching of the theory of evolution in public elementary and secondary schools unless

---

5. 374 U.S. 203 (1963).
6. Ibid., 226 (emphasis added).
7. 107 S. Ct. 2573 (1987).

accompanied by instruction in the theory of "creation science." The act did not require the teaching of either theory unless the other was taught. It defined both of the theories as "the scientific evidences and inferences from those scientific evidences."[8] The act was challenged by various parents, teachers, and religious leaders as violative of the Establishment Clause. The District Court held that the act violated the Establishment Clause. The three-judge Court of Appeals affirmed. The Supreme Court held, in a seven-to-two decision, that the primary purpose of the legislation was to advance a particular religious belief and therefore did not serve any identifiable secular purpose, despite the act's stated secular purpose of promotion of academic freedom.

Justices Brennan, Marshall, Blackmun, and Stevens, all safely predictable separationists, had no difficulty in finding that the Louisiana act had no valid secular purpose. In speaking for the Court, Justice Brennan stated:

> The Creationism Act is designed *either* to promote the theory of creation science which embodies a particular religious tenet by requiring that creation science be taught whenever evolution is taught *or* to prohibit the teaching of a scientific theory disfavored by certain religious sects by forbidding the teaching of evolution when creation science is not also taught. The Establishment Clause, however, forbids *alike* the preference of a religious doctrine *or* the prohibition of theory which is deemed antagonistic to a particular dogma. Because the primary purpose of the Creationism Act is to advance a particular religious belief, the Act endorses religion in violation of the First Amendment.[9]

Justice Scalia and Chief Justice Rehnquist, both safely predictable accommodationists, dissented. Justice Scalia, in his dissenting opinion (joined by Rehnquist), found a legitimate secular purpose in the Louisiana legislation: "to protect academic freedom by providing student choice."[10]

Justice White, who normally lines up on the accommodationist

---

8. Ibid at 2574.
9. Ibid., 2583 (emphasis in original).
10. Ibid., 2602 (Scalia, J., dissenting).

side, nevertheless voted with the majority on deference principles. "We usually defer to the Court of Appeals on the meaning of a state statute, especially when the District Court has the same view. Of course, we have the power to disagree. . . . But if the meaning ascribed to a state statute by a court of appeals is a rational construction of the statute, we normally accept it."[11] White's true sentiments for the case's outcome, however, were not with the majority. He added, "Even if as an original matter I might have arrived at a different conclusion based on a reading of the statute . . . I cannot say that the two courts below are so plainly wrong that they should be reversed."[12]

Justice O'Connor, who more often than not had leaned toward the accommodationists in the years immediately following her 1981 appointment to the Court, but who since 1985 has argued for only a restructuring of the *Lemon* test rather than a complete abandonment, sided with the majority. Agreeing that the Louisiana statute violated the "secular purpose prong," she joined Justice Lewis Powell's concurring opinion, which emphasized that the Court's decision diminished the broad discretion that should be "accorded state and local officials in the selection of the public school curriculum."[13] As safely predictable centrists, Justices O'Connor and Powell tentatively sided with the separationists, but more or less expressed the view that they were not unsympathetic to elements of the accommodationist perspective.

How do the current members of the Supreme Court line up on the separationist–accommodationist–centrist scale? As the decade of the nineties opened, the Court had a solid group of four separationists (Brennan, Marshall, Blackmun, and Stevens). The four were usually firmly committed to a broad interpretation of the Establishment Clause, with only Stevens indicating any periodic reluctance to abide fully by the *Lemon* purpose-effect-entanglement test. The strength of this separationist block was severely eroded, however (or at least it would so appear), when Justice Brennan retired in 1990 for health reasons. His replacement, David Souter, was noncontroversial enough to be

---

11. Ibid., 2592 (White, J., concurring).
12. Ibid.
13. Ibid., 2585 (Powell, J., concurring).

confirmed by the United States Senate, but it is probably safe to expect that he will be, on church-state issues, either an accommodationist or a centrist, but not a separationist. Prior to his appointment, Souter never adjudicated a church-state case while serving five years on the bench of the Superior Court of New Hampshire and seven years on the New Hampshire Supreme Court.[14] His basic judicial philosophy and temperament, however, are clearly more conservative than his predecessor's, and the Senate confirmation hearings made this clear. The separationist block has thus been reduced to three, and given Justice Stevens's periodic wavering, the block may actually be at less than three-man strength.

Chief Justice Rehnquist and Justices Scalia and White comprise a predictably accommodationist block, notwithstanding White's willingness to vote with the majority in *Aguillard*. As a group, they tend to find constitutional support for almost any kind of accommodation, provided they can detect *some* kind of secular purpose—and, arguably, one can usually be found. For all three justices the *Lemon* test leads to unprincipled results and should be revamped if not totally scrapped, an attitude not particularly surprising in light of their view that the Establishment Clause demands little more than no preference of any religion.

Justice O'Connor remains clearly a centrist, choosing to work within the parameters of the *Lemon* test on a case-by-case basis. While it is still too early to make any permanent judgments about the church-state views of Anthony Kennedy (the replacement of the retired Justice Powell), the early signs are that the confirming Senate's perception of him as a probable centrist may prove to be erroneous. Thus far, he has sided repeatedly with the accommodationist block on the Court. Moreover, in the 1989 case of *Allegheny* v. *ACLU*,[15] in which he dissented from the majority's finding that a crèche in the county courthouse in Pittsburgh displayed next to a banner bearing the inscription "Gloria in Excelsis Deo" violated the Establishment Clause,

---

14. Rob Boston, "Is Souter Suitable?" *Church and State* 43 (September 1990): 4.

15. 109 S. Ct. 3086 (1989).

he criticized the majority, in language similar to that frequently used by other accommodationists on the Court, as harboring a "latent hostility"[16] or "callous indifference"[17] toward religion.

Kennedy, however, in the same *Allegheny* case, was less hostile to the *Lemon* test, if only slightly, than Rehnquist, Scalia, and White have been. Noting that persuasive criticism of the *Lemon* test had emerged on the Court, he stated that he was "content for present purposes to remain within the *Lemon* framework,"[18] but that he did not "wish to be seen as advocating, let alone adopting, that test as [the] primary guide in this difficult area."[19]

The crucial significance of Justice O'Connor as a centrist and Justices Kennedy and Souter as, say, "conservative" centrists is obvious—they can make a successful majority for either the separationists or the accommodationists. It appears likely that the Court, as in the *Allegheny* case, will decide numerous church-state cases in the immediate future on razor-thin five-to-four margins,[20] it being anyone's guess as to what principles the majority will look to for their decisions.

16. Ibid., 3135.
17. Ibid., 3138.
18. Ibid., 3134.
19. Ibid.
20. Also illustrative is the case of *Bowen* v. *Kendrick*, 108 S. Ct. 2562 (1988), where the Court rendered an accommodationist decision by a narrow five-to-four vote. With Chief Justice Rehnquist writing for the majority, the Court held that the Adolescent Health Services and Pregnancy Prevention and Care Act, passed by Congress in 1978, did not violate the Establishment Clause. The legislation was designed primarily to provide aid to various public and private organizations that could, in turn, assist teenagers in the prevention of sexual activity and pregnancy. The legislation was challenged because some of the recipients of grants under the act maintained close ties with sectarian religious organizations, and because there was evidence that some of the recipients rendered sectarian-based religious counseling. The Court found that the legislation did not violate the *Lemon* test on its face despite the fact that funds could be granted to organizations with close sectarian connections. The Court did, however, remand the case to the district court for a determination of whether some of the recipients were improperly advancing religion. Justices White, Scalia, O'Connor, and Kennedy joined Rehnquist in the Court's opinion; Justice Blackmun's dissenting opinion was joined by Justices Marshall, Brennan, and Stevens.

The Leadership and Influence of Rehnquist as Chief Justice

Given the potential for close votes in future church-state cases, one might naturally wonder about the ability of William Rehnquist to influence the Supreme Court's direction by virtue of his position as chief justice. The position of chief justice does offer opportunities for significant influence in two primary areas: Supreme Court conferences and opinion assignments.

Supreme Court Conferences

As presiding officer of the closed Supreme Court conference, the chief justice enjoys important initiating powers with respect to all Court cases. William Howard Taft, who served the country as President from 1909 to 1913, served a decade later as Chief Justice of the Supreme Court, and observed that the occupant of that office "is the head of the Court, and while his vote counts but one of the nine, he is, if he be a man of strong and persuasive personality, abiding convictions, recognized by learning and statesmanlike foresight, expected to promote team-work by the Court, so as to give weight and solidarity to its opinions."[21]

The Supreme Court conference is a meeting at which cases are discussed by the Court members, both before and after oral arguments. Before oral arguments are heard, the facts and relevant legal issues for pending cases are discussed with the chief justice presiding over the discussion. After oral arguments, the customary procedure is for the chief justice to open the conference by giving a comprehensive summary of the case, followed by a statement of his view of the case and his rationale for that view. Thus he is in a position to influence decisively the outcome of a case, especially if there are a number of justices who are undecided on a case. As one writer has noted in connection with the "genuine power" of the chief justice in conference, "In any discussion the first analysis of a problem will

---

21. Quoted in Peter G. Fish, *The Office of Chief Justice* (Charlottesville, Va.: The White Burkett Miller Center of Public Affairs, 1984), 23.

more often than not affect the analysis of anyone else. The man who selects the issues to be talked about very frequently dominates the end result."[22]

Opinion Assignments

The chief justice, when in the majority, exercises the prerogative of assigning the drafting of Court opinions—a prerogative that can significantly determine what the Court's opinion will say. Yet even when there is no clear-cut majority on a case, the chief justice can influence the final vote. Typically, when a straw-vote is taken and no majority manifests itself, the chief justice will assign to one justice of his selection the task of preparing a memorandum on the case. Other justices are also invited to prepare memorandums, but the one assigned memorandum is frequently influential in forming a Court consensus.

The assigning of opinion authorship, Princeton's Alpheus T. Mason has declared,

> offers almost boundless possibilities for the Chief Justice to exert his influence. He can use it to advance his own prestige, taking the plums for himself, leaving the dry, inconsequential cases to his colleagues. The Chief Justice may exercise it so as to exploit the special talents of his Associate Justices, or use it in such a way as to develop specialties they do not already possess. He can use the opinion-signing function to give added weight to a particular decision. . . . In a controversial case, he can use the assignment power to promote harmony by selecting a writer other than the obvious spokesman of the Court's divergent wings, or add to judicial asperities by singling out the previously vehement dissenter to voice the view now held by a majority. . . .[23]

---

22. John P. Frank, *Marble Palace: The Supreme Court in American Life* (New York: Knopf, 1958), 75, quoted in Fish, *The Office*, 28.

23. Alpheus T. Mason, "Chief Justice of the United States: Primus Inter Pares," *Journal of Public Law* 17 (1968): 26, quoted in Fish, *The Office*, 28.

Mason concludes that, in strategically exercising these prerogatives, a chief justice "will not only affect the dispatch of judicial business but may vitally influence the course of law and history."[24]

Given the prerogatives accorded Chief Justice Rehnquist as the Court's presiding officer, his influence could be considerable in future church-state cases, especially in view of the close split on church-state philosophy that prevails on the Court. Every justice forms his vote independently, of course, but that independent vote is rarely shaped in isolation from the influence of other justices—and especially not in isolation from the chief justice.

Concluding Remarks

The separationist-accommodationist controversy defies easy analysis or resolution. Each side offers with persuasive certitude its own interpretation of what the framers intended by those revered sixteen words: "Congress shall make no law respecting an establishment of religion, or prohibiting the free exercise thereof." The heightened level of the controversy may, however, be a blessing in disguise. If it drives the guardians of American church-state relations—professors, scholars, lawyers, judges, and politicians—to deeper searches for the "original intent" of the framers, the outcome will likely be a fuller understanding of the foundation for the doctrine of the separation of church and state: the fundamental principles of religious liberty that developed and matured during the approximate period of 1630-1830.

The "original intent" of the framers must be seen in the context of the two-hundred-year revolution for religious liberty. The framing of the Constitution and the Bill of Rights occurred at a stage in the revolution when the principles of separation had not yet reached full actualization. As a result, the religion clauses cannot be read and interpreted—then or now—as being a complete statement of the proper relationship between church and state. The principles of separation were coming to full bloom in 1789 in many of the states—Virginia

---

24. Ibid.

was most representative because of the profound articulations of Jefferson and Madison—yet many of the states were not as far along the path toward full religious liberty. As a result, the First Amendment prohibited only the federal government's jurisdiction over religious matters, not that of the states. Eventually, however, all of the states caught the vision for full religious liberty, and abandoned their church-state unions.

The religion clauses are not crystalline. Their phrasing is broad and their limitations are not clearly marked. That a full comprehension of religious liberty was not yet attained across the states in 1789 is reflected in the religion clauses. There probably was not total agreement among the framers on what was meant by "an establishment of religion," or the "free exercise thereof." As a result, the framers differences are hidden in cloaks of generality. Yet the basic principles of full religious liberty are seen in the clauses—the clear notion of separation lay just beneath the thin veneer of ambiguity. Chief Justice Warren Burger recognized this in stating that the goal of the framers in drawing the religion clauses was "to state an objective, not to write a statute."[25] That objective was to prohibit government involvement, support, and restraint of religion—a separation of the spheres of religion and civil authority.

Even if William Rehnquist and other accommodationists are correct in asserting that the basic goal of the framers was to prohibit a national church or the preferential treatment of some religious groups over others, that understanding should not prevent the absorption and implementation of the fuller expressions of religious liberty that were to come to maturity after 1789. If, for example, the definition of an "establishment" of religion broadened after 1789—and it did—to take on the multiple meanings of that term so clearly pronounced in, for example, Madison's "Remonstrance," then that development should be acknowledged by constitutional interpreters in preference to clinging to a static meaning of an "establishment" that prevailed when the First Amendment was fashioned. In this respect, what constitutional fundamentals meant to the wisdom of past times cannot

---

25. *Walz v. Tax Commission of New York*, 397 U.S. 664 (1970), 668.

be the sole vision to later times. This realization is not a novel one. To quote from one of the Supreme Court's early opinions of this century:

> Time works changes, brings into existence new conditions and purposes. Therefore a principle to be vital must be capable of wider application than the mischief which gave it birth. This is peculiarly true of constitutions. They are not ephemeral enactments, designed to meet passing occasions. They are, to use the words of Chief Justice Marshall, "designed to approach immortality as nearly as human institutions can approach it." The future is their care and provision for events of good and bad tendencies of which no prophecy can be made. In the application of a constitution, therefore, our contemplation cannot be only of what has been but of what may be.[26]

Constitutional interpretation cannot always be bound to the "original intent" of the framers, especially when it is not clear. As William Brennan has said, "Our Constitution was not intended to preserve a preexisting society but to make a new one, to put in place new principles that the prior political community had not sufficiently recognized."[27] Thus, even if a mature doctrine of church-state separation was not envisioned by the framers, but there later developed a broadly accepted doctrine of church-state separation, then American church-state relations must be built upon the newer vision. There was, to be sure, a vision of separation in America; it was simply in adolescence when the First Amendment was written, and did not reach adulthood until the 1830s.

The vision of separation is validated not only by the First Amendment, but by history itself. Alexis de Tocqueville, the French journalist and historian who traveled extensively in the United States in the 1830s, observed that "the religious atmosphere of the country was the first thing that struck me on my arrival in the United States." He expressed "astonishment" because in his familiar Europe religion and freedom marched "in opposite directions." After questioning

---

26. *Weems v. United States*, 217 U.S. 349 (1910), 373.
27. Brennan Speech, 438.

pastors, priests, and laymen from all of the denominations and sects he encountered, he found that "they all agreed with each other except about the details; all thought that the quiet sway of religion over their country was *the complete separation of church and state*. I have no hesitation in stating that throughout my stay in America I met nobody, lay or cleric, who did not agree about that."[28]

The accommodationist impulse in contemporary America is, it is hoped, unlikely to make a permanent impression. An absolutist Supreme Court on the side of accommodationism, even if it were to take form, would encounter serious difficulties. It is not likely that the American public would easily take to a stepped-up erosion of the principles of religious liberty that have thrived for two hundred years.

Granted, a measure of accommodation is likely to continue—there has always been an acceptable level. Thus it is entirely probable that the Court will continue to allow religious symbols, chaplaincies, legislative prayers, and some aid to parochial education. A full-scale accommodationism, however, with nonpreferential aid to all churches, parochial schools, and religious exercises in public schools, and especially blatant denials of religious liberty along the lines of the *Smith* result, as examples, would encounter strong resistance. The public outcry, no doubt, would be thunderous. Such an upscaling of accommodationism might also be a blessing in disguise—the infringements on religious liberty would be all too conspicuous, and an American people steeped in the tradition of separation of church and state very likely would make the necessary corrections in democratic course.

Yet, realistically, the anticipation that separationism as a treasured principle of religious liberty in America will be recaptured even if lost temporarily, is mere conjecture. If lost, it might in fact never be recaptured. As Justice Wiley Rutledge stated in his dissent in *Everson*, "Like St. Paul's freedom, religious liberty with a great price must be bought,"[29] and in a democracy, a great part of that price is always

---

28. Alexis de Tocqueville, *Democracy in America*, ed. J. P. Mayers and Max Lerner, trans. George Lawrence (New York: Harper & Row, 1969), 271-72 (emphasis added).
    29. 330 U.S. 1 (1947), 59.

a commitment by the citizenry to remain informed and politically involved. The preservation of religious liberty in the United States always will demand vigilance and dedicated resolve by its greatest protectors, the American people.

Separationism grounds its claims in the founding fathers, but so does accommodationism. Retired Justice William Brennan, for one, traces his separationist perspective to the framers, but Chief Justice William Rehnquist likewise traces his accommodationism to the framers. Who is right and who is wrong? While neither can be completely right, probably neither is completely wrong. As one distinguished author has written: "We live in an imperfect constitutional universe cluttered with ambiguities, mysteries, and inconsistencies. History confounds us. It is delphic and scorns those who seek clarity, certainty, and consistency."[30]

William Rehnquist claims to be a First Amendment restorationist—one who restores the amendment's true meaning. Yet, a restorationist would explicate history so as to clear up misconceptions. Unfortunately, as has been explained, the limited period of history examined by Rehnquist is not clear enough to provide an adequate explication of the meaning of the religion clauses. Rehnquist's understanding of the religion clauses is flawed because he looks almost exclusively to the proceedings of the First Congress for his understanding. He fails to see the broad sweep of the revolution for full religious liberty, the movement for the complete separation of church and state, of which the proceedings of the First Congress were only a small—and, if isolated, ambiguous—part.

In contrast, the Supreme Court, in the early cases of *Everson*, *McCollum*, *Engel*, and *Schempp* astutely perceived the early vision for separation, best articulated by Jefferson and Madison in the Virginia drive for full religious liberty, and incorporated that vision in its interpretations of the religion clauses. William Brennan, for one, as well as the separationists now serving on the Supreme Court maintain that vision. William Rehnquist and the other accommodationists now serving on the Court erode that vision. The former, and not the latter,

---

30. Leonard Levy, *The Establishment Clause*, xiv.

are the true restorationists.

If Rehnquist is not a restorationist, how then should he be characterized? When asked to describe his basic judicial philosophy in the 1971 Senate nomination hearings, Rehnquist replied, "Fidelity to the Constitution and let the chips fall where they may."[31] He has remained true to that philosophy, even in the face of a steady flow of criticism against him and his views. In spite of his abbreviated view of history, Chief Justice Rehnquist is, nonetheless, a constitutionalist. As a constitutionalist he seeks to examine the Constitution, and with all of his capacities, uphold it. No person who has examined William Rehnquist as a man, scholar, and jurist holding this nation's highest judicial office could ever assert that he seeks to do anything less. In so doing, he serves well his office and his country.

---

31. 1971 *Nomination Hearings*, 156.

APPENDIX A

A Bill for Establishing Religious Freedom

[Jefferson presented this bill to the Virginia Assembly in June 1779. It was adopted by the Assembly in 1785 and became law 16 January 1786.]

Well aware that the opinions and belief of men depend not on their own will, but follow involuntarily the evidence proposed to their own minds; that Almighty God hath created the mind free, and manifested his supreme will that free it shall remain by making it altogether insusceptible of restraint; that all attempts to influence it by temporal punishments, or burthens, or by civil incapacitations, tend only to beget habits of hypocrisy and meanness, and are a departure from the plan of the holy author of our religion, who being lord both of body and mind, yet chose not to propagate it by coercions on either, as was in his Almighty power to do, but to extend it by its influence on reason alone; civil as well as ecclesiastical, who, being themselves but fallible and uninspired men, have assumed dominion over the faith of others, setting up their own opinions and modes of thinking as the only true and infallible, and as such endeavoring to impose them on others, hath established and maintained false religions over the greatest part of the world and through all time: That to compel a man to furnish contributions

Reprinted from *The Papers of Thomas Jefferson*, ed. Julian P. Boyd, 20 vols. to date (Princeton, N.J.: Princeton University Press, 1950-   ) 2:545-46.

of money for the propagation of opinions which he disbelieves and abhors, is sinful and tyrannical; that even the forcing him to support this or that teacher of his own religious persuasion, is depriving him of the comfortable liberty of giving his contributions to the particular pastor whose morals he would make his pattern, and whose powers he feels most persuasive to righteousness; and is withdrawing from the ministry those temporary rewards, which proceeding from an approbation of their personal conduct, are an additional incitement to earnest and unremitting labours for the instruction of mankind; that our civil rights have no dependance on our religious opinions, any more than our opinions in physics or geometry; that therefore the proscribing any citizen as unworthy the public confidence by laying upon him an incapacity of being called to offices of trust and emolument, unless he profess or renounce this or that religious opinion, is depriving him injuriously of those privileges and advantages to which, in common with his fellow citizens, he has a natural right; that it tends also to corrupt the principles of that very religion it is meant to encourage, by bribing, with a monopoly of worldly honours and emoluments, those who will externally profess and conform to it; that though indeed these are criminal who do not withstand such temptation, yet neither are those innocent who lay the bait in their way; that the opinions of men are not the object of civil government, nor under its jurisdiction; that to suffer the civil magistrate to intrude his powers into the field of opinion and to restrain the profession or propagation of principles on supposition of their ill tendency is a dangerous fallacy, which at once destroys all religious liberty, because he being of course judge of that tendency will make his opinions the rule of judgment, and approve or condemn the sentiments of others only as they shall square with or differ from his own; that it is time enough to interfere when principles break out into overt acts against peace and good order; and finally, that truth is great and will prevail if left to herself; that she is the proper and sufficient antagonist to error, and has nothing to fear from the conflict unless by human interposition disarmed of her natural weapons, free argument and debate; errors ceasing to be dangerous when it is permitted freely to contradict them.

We the General Assembly of Virginia do enact that no man shall be compelled to frequent or support any religious worship, place, or ministry whatsoever, nor shall be enforced, restrained, molested, or burthened in his body or goods, nor shall otherwise suffer, on account of his religious opinions or belief; but that all men shall be free to profess, and by argument to maintain, their opinions in matters of religion, and that the same shall in no wise diminish, enlarge, or affect their civil capacities.

And though we will know that this Assembly, elected by the people for the ordinary purposes of legislation only, have no power to restrain the acts of succeeding Assemblies, constituted with powers equal to our own, and that therefore to declare this act irrevocable would be of no effect in law; yet we are free to declare, and do declare, that the rights hereby asserted are of the natural rights of mankind, and that if any act shall be hereafter passed to repeal the present or to narrow its operation, such act will be an infringement of natural right.

APPENDIX B

A Memorial and Remonstrance Against Religious Assessments

1785

[This memorial, written by James Madison, was instrumental in the defeat of a proposal in the Virginia House of Delegates to provide assessments to be used for the teaching of religion.]

We the subscribers, citizens of the said Commonwealth, having taken into serious consideration, a Bill printed by order of the last Session of General Assembly, entitled "A Bill establishing a provision for Teachers of the Christian Religion," and conceiving that the same if finally armed with the sanctions of a law, will be a dangerous abuse of power, are bound as faithful members of a free State to remonstrate against it, and to declare the reasons by which we are determined. We remonstrate against the said Bill.

1. Because we hold it for a fundamental and undeniable truth, "that Religion or the duty which we owe to our Creator and the manner of discharging it, can be directed only by reason and conviction, not by

Reprinted from *The Papers of James Madison*, eds. William T. Hutchinson and William M. E. Rachal (Chicago: University of Chicago Press, 1962-   ) 8: 298-304.

force or violence." The Religion then of every man must be left to the conviction and conscience of every man; and it is the right of every man to exercise it as these may dictate. This right is in its nature an unalienable right. It is unalienable, because the opinions of men, depending only on the evidence contemplated by their own minds cannot follow the dictates of other men: It is unalienable also, because what is here a right towards men, is a duty towards the Creator. It is the duty of every man to render to the Creator such homage and such only as he believes to be acceptable to him. This duty is precedent, both in order of time and in degree of obligation, to the claims of Civil Society. Before any man can be considered as a member of Civil Society, he must be considered as a Subject of the Governor of the Universe: And if a member of Civil Society, who enters into any subordinate Association, must always do it with a reservation of his duty to the General Authority; much more must every man who becomes a member of any particular Civil Society, do it with a saving of his allegiance to the Universal Sovereign. We maintain therefore that in matters of Religion, no mans right is abridged by the institution of Civil Society and that Religion is wholly exempt from its cognizance. True it is, that no other rule exists, by which any question which may divide a Society, can be ultimately determined, but the will of the majority; but it is also true that the majority may trespass on the rights of the minority.

2. Because if Religion be exempt from the authority of the Society at large, still less can it be subject to that of the Legislative Body. The latter are but the creatures and vicegerents of the former. Their jurisdiction is both derivative and limited: It is limited with regard to the co-ordinate departments, more necessarily is it limited with regard to the constituents. The preservation of a free Government requires not merely, that the metes and bounds which separate each department of power be invariably maintained; but more especially that neither of them be suffered to overleap the great Barrier which defends the rights of the people. The Rulers who are guilty of such an encroachment, exceed the commission from which they derive their authority, and are Tyrants. The People who submit to it are governed by laws made neither by themselves nor by an authority derived from them, and are slaves.

3. Because it is proper to take alarm at the first experiment on our liberties. We hold this prudent jealousy to be the first duty of Citizens,

and one of the noblest characteristics of the late Revolution. The free men of America did not wait till usurped power had strengthened itself by exercise, and entangled the question in precedents. They saw all the consequences in the principle, and they avoided the consequences by denying the principle. We revere this lesson too much soon to forget it. Who does not see that the same authority which can establish Christianity, in exclusion of all other Religions, may establish with the same ease any particular sect of Christians, in exclusion of all other Sects? That the same authority which can force a citizen to contribute three pence only of his property for the support of any one establishment, may force him to conform to any other establishment in all cases whatsoever?

4. Because the Bill violates that equality which ought to be the basis of every law, and which is more indispensable, in proportion as the validity or expediency of any law is more liable to be impeached. If "all men are by nature equally free and independent," all men are to be considered as entering into Society on equal conditions; as relinquishing no more, and therefore retaining no less, one than another, of their natural rights. Above all are they to be considered as retaining an "equal title to the free exercise of Religion according to the dictates of Conscience." Whilst we assert for ourselves a freedom to embrace, to profess and to observe the Religion which we believe to be of divine origin, we cannot deny an equal freedom to those whose minds have not yet yielded to the evidence which has convinced us. If this freedom be abused, it is an offence against God, not against man: To God, therefore, not to man, must an account of it be rendered. As the Bill violates equality by subjecting some to peculiar burdens, so it violates the same principle, by granting to others peculiar exemptions. Are the Quakers and Mennonists the only sects who think a compulsive support of their Religions unnecessary and unwarrantable? Can their piety alone be entrusted with the care of public worship? Ought their Religions to be endowed above all others with extraordinary privileges by which proselytes may be enticed from all others? We think too favorably of the justice and good sense of those denominations to believe that they either covet pre-eminences over their fellow citizens or that they will be seduced by them from the common opposition to the measure.

5. Because the Bill implies either that the Civil Magistrate is a

competent Judge of Religious Truth; or that he may employ Religion as an engine of Civil policy. The first is an arrogant pretension falsified by the contradictory opinions of Rulers in all ages, and throughout the world: the second an unhallowed perversion of the means of salvation.

6. Because the establishment proposed by the Bill is not requisite for the support of the Christian Religion. To say that it is, is a contradiction to the Christian Religion itself, for every page of it disavows a dependence on the powers of this world: it is a contradiction to fact; for it is known that this Religion both existed and flourished, not only without the support of human laws, but in spite of every opposition from them, and not only during the period of miraculous aid, but long after it had been left to its own evidence and the ordinary care of Providence. Nay, it is a contradiction in terms; for a Religion not invented by human policy, must have pre-existed and been supported, before it was established by human policy. It is moreover to weaken in those who profess this Religion a pious confidence in its innate excellence and the patronage of its Author; and to foster in those who still reject it, a suspicion that its friends are too conscious of its fallacies to trust it to its own merits.

7. Because experience witnesseth that ecclesiastical establishments, instead of maintaining the purity and efficacy of Religion, have had a contrary operation. During almost fifteen centuries has the legal establishment of Christianity been on trial. What have been its fruits? More or less in all places, pride and indolence in the Clergy, ignorance and servility in the laity, in both, superstition, bigotry and persecution. Enquire of the Teachers of Christianity for the ages in which it appeared in its greatest lustre; those of every sect, point to the ages prior to its incorporation with Civil policy. Propose a restoration of this primitive State in which its Teachers depended on the voluntary rewards of their flocks, many of them predict its downfall. On which Side ought their testimony to have greatest weight, when for or when against their interest?

8. Because the establishment in question is not necessary for the support of the Civil Government. If it be urged as necessary for the support of Civil Government only as it is a means of supporting Religion, and it be not necessary for the latter purpose, it cannot be necessary for the former. If Religion be not within the cognizance of Civil Government how can its legal establishment be necessary to Civil Government? What influence in fact have ecclesiastical establishments had on Civil Society?

In some instances they have been seen to erect a spiritual tyranny on the ruins of the Civil authority; in many instances they have been seen upholding the thrones of political tyranny; in no instance have they been seen the guardians of the liberties of the people. Rulers who wished to subvert the public liberty, may have found an established Clergy convenient auxiliaries. A just Government instituted to secure and perpetuate it needs them not. Such a Government will be best supported by protecting every Citizen in the enjoyment of his Religion with the same equal hand which protects his person and his property; by neither invading the equal rights of any Sect, not suffering any Sect to invade those of another.

9. Because the proposed establishment is a departure from that generous policy, which, offering an Asylum to the persecuted and oppressed of every Nation and Religion, promised a lustre to our country, and an accession to the number of its citizens. What a melancholy mark is the Bill of sudden degeneracy? Instead of holding forth an Asylum to the persecuted, it is itself a signal of persecution. It degrades from the equal rank of Citizens all those whose opinions in Religion do not bend to those of the Legislative authority. Distant as it may be in its present form from the Inquisition, it differs from it only in degree. The one is the first step, the other the last in the career of intolerance. The magnanimous sufferer under this cruel scourge in foreign Religions, must view the Bill as a Beacon on our Coast, warning him to seek some other haven, where liberty and philanthropy in their due extent, may offer a more certain repose from his Troubles.

10. Because it will have a like tendency to banish our Citizens. The allurements presented by other situations are every day thinning their number. To superadd a fresh motive to emigration by revoking the liberty which they now enjoy, would be the same species of folly which has dishonoured and depopulated flourishing kingdoms.

11. Because it will destroy that moderation and harmony which the forbearance of our laws to intermeddle with Religion has produced among its several sects. Torrents of blood have been spilt in the old world, by vain attempts of the secular arm, to extinguish Religious discord, by proscribing all difference in religious opinion. Time has at length revealed the true remedy. Every relaxation of narrow and rigorous policy, wherever it has been tried, has been found to assuage the disease. The American Theatre has exhibited proofs that equal and compleat liberty, if it does

not wholly eradicate it, sufficiently destroys its malignant influence on the health and prosperity of the State. If with the salutary effects of this system under our own eyes, we begin to contract the bounds of Religious freedom, we know no name that will too severely reproach our folly. At least let warning be taken at the first fruits of the threatened innovation. The very appearance of the Bill has transformed "that Christian forbearance, love and charity," which of late mutually prevailed, into animosities and jealousies, which may not soon be appeased. What mischiefs may not be dreaded, should this enemy to the public quiet be armed with the force of a law?

12. Because the policy of the Bill is adverse to the diffusion of the light of Christianity. The first wish of those who enjoy this precious gift ought to be that it may be imparted to the whole race of mankind. Compare the number of those who have as yet received it with the number still remaining under the dominion of false Religions; and how small is the former! Does the policy of the Bill tend to lessen the disproportion? No; it at once discourages those who are strangers to the light of revelation from coming into the Religion of it; and countenances by example the nations who continue in darkness, in shutting out those who might convey it to them. Instead of levelling as far as possible, every obstacle to the victorious progress of Truth, the Bill with an ignoble and unchristian timidity would circumscribe it with a wall of defence against the encroachments of errors.

13. Because attempts to enforce by legal sanctions, acts obnoxious to so great a proportion of Citizens, tend to enervate the laws in general, and to slacken the bands of Society. If it be difficult to execute any law which is not generally deemed necessary or salutary, what must be the case, where it is deemed invalid and dangerous? And what may be the effect of so striking an example of impotency in the Government, on its general authority?

14. Because a measure of such singular magnitude and delicacy ought not to be imposed, without the clearest evidence that it is called for by a majority of citizens, and no satisfactory method is yet proposed by which the voice of the majority in this case may be determined, or its influence secured. "The people of the respective counties are indeed requested to signify their opinion respecting the adoption of the Bill to the next Session of Assembly." But the representation must be made

equal, before the voice either of the Representatives of the Counties will be that of the people. Our hope is that neither of the former will, after due consideration, espouse the dangerous principle of the Bill. Should the event disappoint us, it will still leave us in full confidence, that a fair appeal to the latter will reverse the sentence against our liberties.

15. Because finally, "the equal right of every citizen to the free exercise of his Religion according to the dictates of conscience" is held by the same tenure with all our other rights. If we recur to its origin, it is equally the gift of nature; if we weigh its importance, it cannot be less dear to us; if we consult the "Declaration of those rights which pertain to the good people of Virginia, as the basis and foundation of Government," it is enumerated with equal solemnity, or rather studied emphasis. Either then, we must say, that the Will of the Legislature is the only measure of their authority; and that in the plentitude of this authority, they may sweep away all our fundamental rights; or, that they are bound to leave this particular right untouched and sacred: Either we must say, that they may control the freedom of the press, may abolish the Trial by jury, may swallow up the Executive and Judiciary Powers of the State; nay that they may despoil us of our very right of suffrage, and erect themselves into an independent and hereditary Assembly or, we must say, that they have no authority to enact into law the Bill under consideration. We the Subscribers say, that the General Assembly of this Commonwealth have no such authority: And that no effort may be omitted on our part against so dangerous an usurpation, we oppose to it, this remonstrance; earnestly praying, as we are in duty bound, that the Supreme Lawgiver of the Universe, by illuminating those to whom it is addressed, may on the one hand, turn their Councils from every act which would affront his holy prerogative, or violate the trust committed to them: and on the other, guide them into every measure which may be worthy of his [blessing, may re]dound to their own praise; and may establish more firmly the liberties, the prosperity and the happiness of the Commonwealth.

SELECTED BIBLIOGRAPHY

Primary Sources

Book by William Rehnquist

Rehnquist, William H. *The Supreme Court: The Way It Was—The Way It Is* (New York: William Morrow, 1987).

Articles by William Rehnquist

Rehnquist, William H. "All Discord, Harmony Not Understood: The Performance of the Supreme Court of the United States." *Arizona Law Journal* 22 (Winter 1980): 1973-86.

———. "Civility and Freedom of Speech." *Indiana Law Journal* 49 (Fall 1973): 1-7.

———. "First Amendment: Freedom, Philosophy, and the Law." *Gonzaga Law Review* 12 (Fall 1976): 1-18.

———. "Government by Cliché." *Missouri Law Review* 45 (Summer 1980): 379-94.

———. "Is an Expanded Right of Privacy Consistent With Fair and Effective Law Enforcement? Or, Privacy, You've Come a Long Way Baby." *Kansas Law Review* 23 (Fall 1974): 1-22.

———. "Point, Counterpoint: The Evolution of American Political Philosophy." *Vanderbilt Law Review* 34 (March 1981): 249-64.

———. "Political Battles for Judicial Independence." *Washington Law Review* 50 (August 1975): 835-51.

———. "Sense and Nonsense About Judicial Ethics." *Record* 28 (November 1973): 694-713.

Rehnquist, William H. "Subdivision Trusts and the Bankruptcy Act." *Arizona Law Review* 3 (Winter 1961): 165-76.

———. "The Arizona Bar Admission Cases: A Strange Judicial Aberration." *American Bar Association Journal* 44 (March 1958): 229-32.

———. "The Changing Role of the Supreme Court." *Florida State University Law Review* 14 (Spring 1986): 1-14.

———. "The Notion of a Living Constitution." *Texas Law Review* 54 (May 1976): 693-706.

———. "The Old Order Changeth: The Department of Justice Under John Mitchell." *Arizona Law Review* 12 (Summer 1970): 251-59.

———. "The Supreme Court: Past and Present." *American Bar Association Journal* 59 (April 1973): 361-64.

———. "Whither the Courts." *American Bar Association Journal* 60 (July 1974): 787-90.

———. "Who Writes Decisions of the Supreme Court?" *U.S. News and World Report* 79 (13 December 1959): 27-30.

Government Documents

Nominations of William H. Rehnquist and Lewis F. Powell, Jr.: Hearings Before the Senate Judiciary Committee, 92d Congress, First Session (1971).

Nominations of William H. Rehnquist (for Chief Justice) and Antonin Scalia (for Associate Justice): Hearings Before the Senate Judiciary Committee, 99th Congress, First Session (1986).

Public Statutes at Large. Vol. 1. First Congress, Session 1, Chapter 8. "An Act to Provide for the Government of the Territory Northwest of the River Ohio."

Tansill, Charles L., ed. *Documents Illustrative of the Formation of the Union of the American States.* Washington, D.C.: Government Printing Office, 1927.

United States Code (1976 Edition).

Historical Documents

Annals of the Congress of the United States, *The Debates and Proceedings in the Congress of the United States.* 42 vols. Compiled from authentic materials by Joseph Gates, Sr. Washington, D.C.: Gales and Seaton, 1834.

DePauw, Linda Grant, ed. *Documentary History of the First Federal Congress of the United States of America.* 3 vols. Baltimore: Johns Hopkins University Press, 1977.

Elliott, Jonathan. *The Debates in the Several State Conventions on the Adoption of* the Federal Constitution. 5 vols. 2nd ed. Philadelphia: J. P. Lippincott, 1988.

Fleet, Elizabeth, ed. "Madison's Detached Memoranda." William and Mary Quarterly 3 (1946): 554-59.

Hamilton, Alexander. "Opinion on the Constitutionality of an Act to Establish a Bank" (1971). Reprinted in Papers of Alexander Hamilton. Ed. Harold C. Syrett. New York: Columbia University Press, 1961.

Locke, John. "A Letter Concerning Toleration" (1685). Reprinted in Main Currents of Western Thought. 4th ed. Ed. Franklin Le Van Baumer. New Haven, Conn.: Yale University Press, 1978.

Madison, James. Notes of Debates in the Federal Convention of 1787. Ed. Adrianne Koch. Athens, Ohio: Ohio University Press, 1966.

Madison, James, to Thomas Ritchie, letter of 15 September 1791. Reprinted in The Founder's Constitution. 5 vols. Ed. Philip B. Kurland and Ralph Lerner. Chicago: University of Chicago Press, 1987, 1: ch. 2, no. 28, p. 74.

Rutland, Robert A., ed. The Papers of James Madison. 9 vols. Charlottesville, Va.: University of Virginia Press, 1976.

Secondary Sources

Books

Antieu, Chester James, Arthur L. Downey, and Edward C. Roberts. Freedom from Federal Establishment Formation and Early History of the First Amendment Religion Clauses. Milwaukee, Wis.: Bruce Publishing Company, 1964.

Berger, Raoul. Government by Judiciary. Cambridge, Mass.: Harvard University Press, 1977.

Berns, Walter. The First Amendment and the Future of American Democracy. New York: Basic Books, 1976.

Boles, Donald E. Mr. Justice Rehnquist, Judicial Activist: The Early Years. Ames, Iowa: Iowa State University Press, 1987.

Bradley, Gerard V. Church-State Relationships in America. Westport, Conn.: Greenwood Press, Inc., 1987.

Cobb, Sanford H. The Rise of Religious Liberty in America: A History. New York: Macmillan, 1902.

Cord, Robert L. Separation of Church and State: Historical Fact and Current Fiction. New York: Lambeth Press, 1982.

Current, Richard N., T. Harry Williams, and Frank Freidel. American History: A Survey. 2nd ed. New York: Alfred A. Knopf, 1966.

Curry, Thomas. The First Freedoms: Church and State in America to the Passage of the First Amendment. Oxford: Oxford University Press, 1986.

Davis, Sue. Justice Rehnquist and the Constitution. Princeton: Princeton University Press, 1989.

Dworkin, Ronald. *Taking Rights Seriously*. Cambridge, Mass.: Harvard University Press, 1977.

Ely, John Hart. *Democracy and Distrust: A Theory of Judicial Review*. Cambridge, Mass.: Harvard University Press, 1980.

Fairman, Charles. *The Fourteenth Amendment and the Bill of Rights*. New York: De Capo Press, 1970.

Fish, Peter G. *The Office of Chief Justice*. Charlottesville, Va.: The White Burkett Miller Center of Public Affairs, 1984.

Friedman, Leon, ed. *The Justices of the United States Supreme Court: Their Lives and Major Opinions*. 5 vols. New York: Chelsea House, 1978.

Halpern, Stephen C., and Charles M. Lamb, eds. *Supreme Court Activism and Restraint*. Lexington, Mass.: D. C. Heath, 1982.

Handy, Robert T. *A Christian America: Protestant Hopes and Historical Realities*. 2nd ed. New York: Oxford University Press, 1984.

House, H. Wayne, ed. *Restoring the Constitution, 1787-1987: Essays in Celebration of the Bicentennial*. Dallas, Tex.: Probe Books, 1987.

Howe, Mark DeWolfe. *The Garden and the Wilderness: Religion and Government in American Constitutional History*. Chicago: University of Chicago Press, 1965.

Kelly, Alfred H., and Winfred A. Harbison. *The American Constitution: Its Origins and Development*. 3rd ed. New York: W. W. Norton, 1963.

Kurland, Philip. *Religion and the Law: Of Church and State and the Supreme Court*. Chicago: Aldine Publishing Co., 1962.

Levy, Leonard W. *The Establishment Clause: Religion and the First Amendment*. New York: Macmillan, 1986.

———. *Original Intent and the Framers' Constitution*. New York: Macmillan, 1988.

Malbin, Michael J. *Religion and Politics: The Intentions of the Authors of the First Amendment*. Washington, D.C.: American Enterprise Institute for Public Policy Research, 1978.

Miller, Charles A. *The Supreme Court and the Uses of History*. Cambridge, Mass.: Belknap Press of Harvard University, 1969.

Miller, Robert T., and Ronald B. Flowers. *Toward Benevolent Neutrality: Church, State and the Supreme Court*. 3rd ed. Waco, Tex.: Baylor University Press, 1987.

O'Neill, J. M. *Religion and Education Under the Constitution*. New York: Harper & Row, 1949.

Pansini, Anthony J. *Niccolo Machiavelli and the United States of America*. Greenvale, N.Y.: Greenvale Press, 1969.

Perry, Michael. *The Constitution, the Courts, and Human Rights*. New Haven, Conn.: Yale University Press, 1982.

Peterson, Merrill D., and Robert C. Vaughan, eds. *The Virginia Statute for Religious Freedom*. Cambridge: Cambridge University Press, 1988.

Pfeffer, Leo. *Church, State, and Freedom*. 2nd ed. Boston, Mass.: Beacon Press, 1967.

———. *Religion, State, and the Burger Court*. Buffalo, N.Y.: Prometheus Books, 1984.

Schwartz, Bernard. *The Bill of Rights: A Documentary History*. New York: Chelsea House, 1971.

Stokes, Anson Phelps. *Church and State in the United States*. 3 vols. New York: Harper & Brothers, 1950.

Story, Joseph. *Commentaries on the Constitution of the United States*. 3 vols. Boston, Mass.: Hilliard, Greay, and Company, 1833.

Swomley, John M. *Religious Liberty and the Secular State*. Buffalo, N.Y.: Prometheus Books, 1987.

Tocqueville, Alexis de. *Democracy in America*, ed. J. P. Myers and Max Lerner. Translated by George Lawrence. New York: Harper & Row, 1969.

Tribe, Laurence H. *American Constitutional Law*. Mineola, N.Y.: Foundation Press, 1978.

Wood, James E., Jr., ed. *Religion and the State: Essays in Honor of Leo Pfeffer*. Waco, Tex.: Baylor University Press, 1985.

———. ed. *Religion, the State, and Education*. Waco, Tex.: Baylor University Press, 1984.

Wood, James E., Jr., E. Bruce Thompson, and Robert T. Miller. *Church and State in Scripture, History, and Constitutional Law*. Waco, Tex.: Baylor University Press, 1958.

Articles

Abraham, Henry J. "Religion, the Constitution, the Court, and Society: Some Contemporary Reflections on Mandates, Words, Human Beings, and the Art of the Possible." In *How Does the Constitution Protect Religious Freedom?* ed. Robert A. Goldwin and Art Kaufman, 15-42. Washington, D.C.: American Enterprise Institute, 1987.

Adler, Renata. "Coup at the Court." *New Republic*, 14 September 1987, 37-44.

Baker, John S. "James Madison and Religious Freedom." *Benchmark* 3 (January-April 1987): 71-78.

Ball, Howard. "The Convergence of Constitutional Law and Politics in the Reagan Administration: The Exhumation of the 'Jurisprudence of Original Intention' Doctrine." *Cumberland Law Review* 17 (Summer 1987): 877-90.

Banning, Lance. "James Madison, the Statute for Religious Freedom, and the Crisis of Republican Convictions." In *The Virginia Statute for Religious Freedom*, ed. Merrill D. Peterson and Robert C. Vaughan, 109-38. Cambridge: Cambridge University Press, 1988.

Berman, Harold J. "Religion and Law: The First Amendment in Historical Perspective." *Emory Law Journal* 35 (Fall 1987): 777-93.

Bickel, Alexander. "The Original Understanding and the Segregation Decision." *Harvard Law Review* 69 (November 1955): 1-65.

"Black Monday Decision." *America* 107 (7 July 1962): 456.

Boles, Donald E. "Religion and the Public Schools in Judicial Review." *Journal of Church and State* 26 (Winter 1984): 55-71.

Boston, Rob. "Is Souter Suitable?" *Church and State* 43 (September 1990): 4.

Bowen, Ezra. "Radical in Conservative Garb." *Time,* 11 August 1986, 71-72.

Brennan, William J., Jr. "The Constitution of the United States: Contemporary Ratification," Address presented at Georgetown University, Washington, D.C., 12 October 1985; reprinted in *South Texas Law Journal* 27 (1986): 433-45.

Chapple, Stephen, and Donald J. Kraus. "Rehnquist-Scalia Combined Effect May Far Exceed Current Predictions." *National Law Journal* 9 (15 September 1986): 24.

Choper, Jesse H. "The Religion Clauses of the First Amendment: Reconciling the Conflict." *University of Pittsburgh Law Review* 41 (Spring 1980): 673-701.

Cord, Robert L. "Correcting the Record." *National Review,* 11 April 1985, 42.

Denvir, John. "Justice Rehnquist and Constitutional Interpretation." *Hastings Law Journal* 34 (May-July 1983): 1011-53.

Esbeck, Carl. "Five Views of Church-State Relations in Contemporary American Thought." *Brigham Young University Law Review* 86 (Fall 1986): 371-404.

Fairman, Charles. "Does the Fourteenth Amendment Incorporate the Bill of Rights? The Original Understanding." *Stanford Law Review* 2 (1949): 5-139.

Fiss, Owen, and Charles Krauthammer. "A Return to the Antebellum Constitution: The Rehnquist Court." *New Republic,* 10 March 1982, 14-21.

Gest, Ted. "Hear Ye: The Rehnquist Court Is Now in Session." *U.S. News and World Report,* 13 October 1986, 10-11.

———. "The Supreme Court With a Smile." *U.S. News and World Report,* 12 January 1987, 23.

Gey, Steve. "Rebuilding the Wall: The Case for a Return to the Strict Interpretation of the Establishment Clause." *Columbia Law Review* 81 (November 1981): 1463-90.

Hitchcock, James. "The Supreme Court and Religion: Historical Overview and Future Prognosis." *Saint Louis University Law Journal* 24 (September 1980): 183-204.

Howard, A. E. "Justice Rehnquist—A Key Fighter in Major Battles." *American Bar Association Journal* 72 (June 1986): 47-48.

Jaffa, Harry V. "What Were the 'Original Intentions' of the Framers of the Constitution of the United States?" *University of Puget Sound Law Review* 10 (Spring 1987): 351-448.

Jenkins, John A. "The Partisan: A Talk with Justice Rehnquist." *New York Times Magazine,* 3 March 1985, 28-35, 88, 100-01.

Kaufman, Irving R. "What Did the Founding Fathers Intend?" *New York Times Magazine,* 23 February 1986, 42-45.

Kleven, Thomas. "The Constitutional Philosophy of Justice William H. Rehnquist." *Vermont Law Review* 8 (Spring 1983): 1-54.

Kurland, Philip B. "The Origins of the Religion Clauses of the Constitution." *William and Mary Law Review* 27 (Special Issue, 1985-86): 839-61.

Laycock, Douglas. "Nonpreferential Aid to Religion: A False-Claim About Original Intent." *William and Mary Law Review* 27 (Special Issue, 1985-86): 875-923.

————. "Original Intent and the Constitution Today." In *The First Freedom: Religion and the Bill of Rights*, ed. James E. Wood, Jr., 87-112. Waco, Tex.: Dawson Institute of Church-State Studies, 1990.

Levy, Leonard W. "The Original Meaning of the Establishment Clause of the First Amendment." In *Religion and the State: Essays in Honor of Leo Pfeffer*, ed. James E. Wood, Jr., 43-83. Waco, Tex.: Baylor University Press, 1985.

Little, David. "Religion and Civil Virtue in America: Jefferson's Statute Reconsidered." In *The Virginia Statute for Religious Freedom*, ed. Merrill D. Peterson and Robert C. Vaughan, 237-55. Cambridge: Cambridge University Press, 1988.

Little, David, Lawrence Rose, and Harold Berman. "The Interaction of Law and Religion." *Mercer Law Review* 31 (Winter 1980): 405-22.

Lord, Lewis J., and Clemens P. Work. "From Lone Dissenter to Chief." *U.S. News and World Report*, 30 June 1986, 18-22.

Marreety, Nancy. "The Populist of the Adversary Society: The Jurisprudence of William Rehnquist." *Journal of Contemporary Law* 13 (Fall 1987): 221-47.

Martz, Larry, Ann McDaniel, and Maggie Malone. "A Pair of a Tory Kind." *Newsweek*, 30 June 1986, 20-21.

Mason, Alpheus T. "Chief Justice of the United States: Primus Inter Pares." *Journal of Public Law* 17 (1968): 22-30.

McConnell, Michael W. "Accommodation of Religion." *1985 Supreme Court Review* (1985): 1-59.

Meese, Edwin. "The Supreme Court of the United States: Bulwark of a Limited Constitution." Address presented to the annual meeting of the American Bar Association in Washington, D.C., 9 July 1985; reprinted in *South Texas Law Journal* 27 (1986): 455-66.

Moore, John Norton. "The Supreme Court and the Relationship Between the 'Establishment' and 'Free Exercise' Clauses." *Texas Law Review* 42 (December 1963): 142-98.

Morrison, Stanley. "Does the Fourteenth Amendment Incorporate the Bill of Rights? The Judicial Interpretation." *Stanford Law Review* 2 (1949): 140-73.

Murray, John Courtney. "Law and Prepossessions." *Law and Contemporary Problems* 14 (Winter 1949): 29-45.

Pfeffer, Leo. "Freedom and/or Separation: The Constitutional Dilemma of the First Amendment." *Minnesota Law Review* 64 (1980): 551-68.

————. "The Unity of the First Amendment Religion Clauses." In *The First Freedom: Religion and the Bill of Rights*, ed. James E. Wood, Jr., 133-66. Waco, Tex.: Dawson Institute of Church-State Studies, 1990.

Phelps, Glenn A., and Timothy A. Martinez. "Brennan v. Rehnquist: The Politics of Constitutional Jurisprudence." *Gonzaga Law Review* 22 (1986-87): 307-25.

Powell, Jefferson H. "The Compleat Jeffersonian: Justice Rehnquist and Federalism." *Yale Law Journal* 91 (1982): 1317-70.

———. "The Original Understanding of Original Intent." *Harvard Law Review* 98 (March 1985): 885-948.

Reimenschneider, John. "The Judicial Philosophy of William H. Rehnquist." *Mississippi Law Journal* 45 (January 1974): 224-45.

Riggs, Robert E., and Thomas D. Proffitt. "The Judicial Philosophy of Justice Rehnquist." *Akron Law Review* 16 (Spring 1983): 555-604.

Ripple, Kenneth F. "The Entanglement Test of the Religion Clauses—A Ten Year Assessment." *UCLA Law Review* 27 (August 1980): 1195-1239.

Rydell, J. R., II. "Mr. Justice Rehnquist and Judicial Self-Restraint." *Hastings Law Journal* 26 (Fall 1975): 875-915.

Sandalow, Terrance. "Constitutional Interpretation." *Michigan Law Review* 79 (April 1981): 1033-56.

Seide, David Z. "Daily Moments of Silence in Public Schools: A Constitutional Analysis." *New York University Law Review* 58 (May 1983): 365-408.

Shapiro, David L. "Mr. Justice Rehnquist: A Preliminary View." *Harvard Law Review* 90 (March 1976): 293-357.

———. "William Hubbs Rehnquist." In *The Justices of the United States Supreme Court: Their Lives and Major Opinions*, vol. 5, ed. Leon Friedman, 109-41. New York: Chelsea House, 1978.

Simon, James F. "Conflict and Leadership: The U.S. Supreme Court from Marshall to Rehnquist." *Vital Speeches* 53 (1 November 1986): 44-48.

Smith, Rodney K. "Getting Off on the Wrong Foot and Back on Again: A Reexamination of the History of the Framing of the Religion Clauses of the First Amendment and a Critique of the *Reynolds* and *Everson* Decisions." *Wake Forest Law Review* 20 (Fall 1984): 569-642.

Stevens, John Paul. "The Supreme Court of the United States: Reflections After a Summer Recess." Address presented to Federal Bar Association meeting in Chicago, Illinois, 24 October 1985; reprinted in *South Texas Law Journal* 27 (1986): 447-53.

Thomas, Evan, and Richard Lavaco. "Reagan's Mr. Right: Rehnquist Is Picked for the Court's Top Job." *Time*, 30 June 1986, 24-30.

"Uproar Over School Prayer—And the Aftermath." *U.S. News and World Report*, 9 July 1962, 42-44.

Van Patten, Jonathan K. "In the End Is the Beginning: An Inquiry Into the Meaning of the Religion Clauses." *Saint Louis University Law Journal* 27 (February 1983): 1-95.

———. "The Battle Over the Constitution: Meese's Jurisprudence of Original Intention and Brennan's Theory of Contemporary Ratification." *Marquette Law Review* 70 (Spring 1987): 389-422.

Whitehead, John W. "William Rehnquist and the Religion Clauses: A Study in Majoritarianism." *The Rutherford Institute* (White Paper), 1986.

Wood, James E., Jr. " 'No Religious Test Shall Ever Be Required': Reflections on the Bicentennial of the U.S. Constitution." *Journal of Church and State* 29 (Spring 1987): 199-208.

————. "Religion and the Public Schools." *Brigham Young University Law Review* 86 (Fall 1986): 349-70.

————. "Religion Sponsored by the State." *Journal of Church and State* 4 (November 1962): 141-49.

Wylie, Pete. "Rehnquist and Scalia: What Impact Will They Have On the U.S. Supreme Court?" *Christianity Today*, 19 September 1986, 38-39.

TABLE OF CASES

United States Supreme Court Cases

Stone v. *Graham*, 449 U.S. 39 (1980) (Rehnquist, J., dissenting).

Thomas v. *Review Board of the Indiana Employment Security Division*, 450 U.S. 707 (1981) (Rehnquist, J., dissenting).

Thornton v. *Caldor*, 105 S. Ct. 2914 (1985) (Rehnquist, J., dissenting without opinion).

Trimble v. *Gordon*, 430 U.S. 762 (1977) (Rehnquist, J., dissenting).

Two Guys from Harrison-Allentown, Inc. v. *McGinley*, 366 U.S. 582 (1961).

Wallace v. *Jaffree*, 105 S. Ct. 2479 (1985) (Rehnquist, J., dissenting).

Walz v. *Tax Commission of the City of New York*, 397 U.S. 644 (1970).

Weber v. *Aetna Casualty & Surety Co.*, 406 U.S. 164 (1972) (Rehnquist, J., dissenting).

Wisconsin v. *Yoder*, 406 U.S. 205 (1972).

Wolman v. *Walter*, 433 U.S. 229 (1977).

Younger v. *Harris*, 401 U.S. 37 (1971).

Zorach v. *Clauson*, 343 U.S. 306 (1952).

Lower Federal Court Case

Berkey v. *Third Avenue Railway Co.*, 155 N.E. 58 (1926).

Index